RAINBOW EDITION

Inside Out

Theodore Clymer

Donald J. Bissett
Gretchen Wulfing

Consultants

William E. Blanton

Irene J. Frazier

Milton D. Jacobson

Ken Johnson

Bonnie I. McCullough

Karen A. Scibinico

Roger W. Shuy

E. Paul Torrance

GINN AND COMPANY

Acknowledgments

Grateful acknowledgment is made to the following publishers, authors, and agents for permission to use and adapt copyrighted materials:

Abelard-Schuman for the text of *Little Wolf* by Ann McGovern. © Copyright 1965 by Ann McGovern. By permission of Abelard-Schuman.

Thomas Y. Crowell for "The Adventures of Sarah Ida," adapted from *Shoeshine Girl* by Clyde Robert Bulla. Copyright © 1975 by Clyde Robert Bulla. By permission of Thomas Y. Crowell.

The Dial Press for the adaptation of *Minnie Maloney & Macaroni* by Mark Alan Stamaty. Copyright © 1976 by Mark Alan Stamaty. Reprinted by permission of The Dial Press for the United States and Canada and of Sheldon Fogelman for the Rest of the World.

Follet Publishing Company for *Dragon Stew* copyright © 1969 by Tom McGowen. Used by permission of Follett Publishing Company, a division of Follett Corporation.

Harper & Row, Publishers, Inc., for the poem "Robert, Who is Often a Stranger to Himself" from *Bronzeville Boys and Girls* by Gwendolyn Brooks. Copyright © 1956 by Gwendolyn Brooks Blakely. By permission of Harper & Row, Publishers, Inc.

Holt, Rinehart and Winston for "A Pocketful of Cricket" from *A Pocketful of Cricket* by Rebecca Caudill. Illustrated by Evaline Ness. Copyright © 1964 by Rebecca Caudill. Reprinted by permission of Holt, Rinehart and Winston, Publishers.

Little, Brown and Company for the adaptation of "George." Copyright © 1956, by Phyllis Rowand. From *George* by Phyllis Rowand, by permission of Little, Brown and Co.

McGraw-Hill Book Company for "Discovering Dinosaurs," "Whatever Happened to All Those Dinosaurs?" and "Solving the Puzzle." All adapted from *Discovering Dinosaurs* by Glenn O. Blough. Copyright © 1960 by Glenn O. Blough. Used with permission of McGraw-Hill Book Company. Also for the poem "When Dinosaurs Were Roaming." Abridged from *A Dozen Dinosaurs* by Richard Armour. Copyright © 1967 by Richard Armour and Paul Galdone. Used with permission of McGraw-Hill Book Company.

G. P. Putnam's Sons for "Dinosaur Differences." Adaptation by permission of G. P. Putnam's Sons from *In the Time of the Dinosaurs* by William Wise. Copyright © 1963 by William Wise.

Also for "Dooly and the Snortsnoot." Adaptation by permission of G. P. Putnam's Sons from *Dooly and the Snortsnoot* by Jack Kent. Copyright © 1972 by Jack Kent.

Random House, Inc., for "How Do We Know about Dinosaurs?" Adapted by permission of Random House, Inc. from *In the Days of the Dinosaurs*, by Roy Chapman Andrews. Copyright © 1959 by Roy Chapman Andrews. Also for "Lonely Maria." Adapted by permission of Pantheon Books, a Division of Random House Inc. from *Lonely Maria*, by Elizabeth Coatsworth. Copyright © 1960 by Pantheon Books, Inc. Also for the poem "Lemons and Apples" from *Woody and Me*, by Mary Neville. Copyright © 1966 by Mary Neville Woodrich and Ronni Solbert. Reprinted by permission of Pantheon Books, a Division of Random House, Inc. and Mary Neville Woodrich.

Simon & Schuster, Inc., for the poem "Worm" from *A Little Book of Little Beasts* by Mary Ann Hoberman. Copyright © 1973, by Mary Ann Hoberman. Reprinted by permission of Simon and Schuster, a Division of Gulf & Western Corporation.

Arnold Spilka for the poem "The Talking Tiger" from his book *A Lion I Can Do Without*. Copyright © 1964 by Arnold Spilka. Used by permission of the author.

Curtis Brown, Ltd., New York, for "The Adventures of Sarah Ida," adapted from *Shoeshine Girl* by Clyde Robert Bulla. Reprinted by permission of Curtis Brown, Ltd. Copyright © 1975 by Clyde Robert Bulla.

Mary Buckley for her story "How the Wife Took Care of Things," adapted from *Cricket Magazine*, January 1977. Used by permission of the author.

Garrard Publishing Company for "Slue-Foot Sue the Rainmaker" which is an adaptation from the book, *Pecos Bill and the Long Lasso,* by Elizabeth and Carl Carmer. Published by arrangement with Garrard Publishing Co., Champaign, Illinois.

Hamish Hamilton Ltd, London, for the adaptation of *Lonely Maria* by Elizabeth Coatsworth. Used by permission of the British publisher.

Lothrop, Lee & Shepard Company for "Fidelia" by Ruth Adams. Adapted by permission of Lothrop, Lee & Shepard Company from *Fidelia* by Ruth Adams. Copyright © 1970 by Ruth

Adams. Also for "Molly Mullett" by Patricia Coombs. Reprinted by permission of Lothrop, Lee & Shepard Company from *Molly Mullett* by Patricia Coombs. Copyright © 1975 by Patricia Coombs.

Macrae Smith Company for the play "Giant of the Timber" by Nellie McCaslin, adapted from her book *Tall Tales and Tall Men*. Used by permission of the publisher.

Mary Britton Miller for the poem "Cat" from her book *Menagerie*. Used by permission of the author.

The Oasis Press for "All or Nothing" by Juan Sauvageau, adapted from his book *Stories That Must Not Die*, Volume Two. Copyright © 1976, Juan Sauvageau. Used by permission of Oasis Press, Austin, Texas 78767.

Maurice O'Connell, Jr., for the poem "How to Tell the Wild Animals" by Carolyn Wells, abridged from her book *Baubles*. Used by permission.

Russell & Volkening, Inc., for the poems "Fish" and "The Folk Who Live in Backward Town," both from *Hello and Good-by* by Mary Ann Hoberman. Reprinted by permission of Russell & Volkening, Inc. as agents for the author. Copyright © 1959 by Mary Ann Hoberman.

The Shoe String Press, Inc., for the song "Old Grumble." Adapted with permission of the author and the publisher from the Second Edition of *Folk Songs of Old New England*, copyright 1974, compiled by Eloise Hibbard Linscott, published as an Archon Book by The Shoe String Press, Inc., Hamden, Connecticut 06514.

Toni Strassman, Author's Representative, for *Molly Mullett* by Patricia Coombs. Copyright © 1975 by Patricia Coombs. Used by permission.

Albert Whitman & Company for "What Mary Jo Wanted" adapted from *What Mary Jo Wanted* by Janice May Udry, copyright 1968 by Janice May Udry. Reprinted by permission of the Albert Whitman Company.

Windmill Productions, Inc., for excerpts on page 117 from *C D B!* by William Steig. Copyright © 1968 by William Steig. Used by permission of the publisher.

World's Work Ltd., England, for the poem "When Dinosaurs Were Roaming," abridged from *A Dozen Dinosaurs* by Richard Armour. Used by permission.

Illustrations and photographs were provided by the following: American Museum of Natural History (216, 217); Tom Cooke (88–99); Courtesy of the Museum of Natural History (225); Guy Dannella (284–300); Blair Drawson (100–116); Len Ebert (260–265); Jack Freas (61); Rosalind Fry (302–337); Jonathan Goell (45); Judy Sue Goodwin (84–85); Diane de Groat (158–180); William Harmuth (267–273); Bruce Hunter—American Museum of Natural History (226); Mark Kelley (117, 258–259); True Kelley (282, 283); Leonard LeRue III (220); Ted Lewin (19); Richard Loehle (20–31); Ray Mason, (198–215); Lady McCrady (156, 157); Jon McIntosh (64–75); Eleanor Mill (120–133); Leslie Morrill (135–155); Joseph Muench (266); Sal Murdocca (134); Chuck Mitchell (274–281); Ted Rand (32–43, 46–60); C. R. Schaff-Museum of Comparative Zoology, Harvard University (230); Joel Snyder (184–197, 218, 219, 221–224, 231–237); Stock Boston (227); Karl W. Struecklen (8–18); Ed Taber (248–257); Sue Thompson (86, 87); Dr. C. Vaurie-American Museum of Natural History (229); Christine Westerberg (239–244); Lane Yerkes (76–83).

The cover and unit introduction pages were designed by Gregory Fossella Associates.

Contents

6

Mirror, Mirror

7

Little Wolf

It is morning.
The sun begins to rise.

The sun rises higher
and higher in the sky.
It shines on all the houses
of the Indian tribe.

The sun wakes up the mother—Flower Wolf.
And the father—Hunt Wolf.
And the old grandfather—Wise Wolf.
And the boy—Little Wolf.

Another day has come.
Flower Wolf will cook.
Hunt Wolf will hunt.
Wise Wolf will sit by the fire.

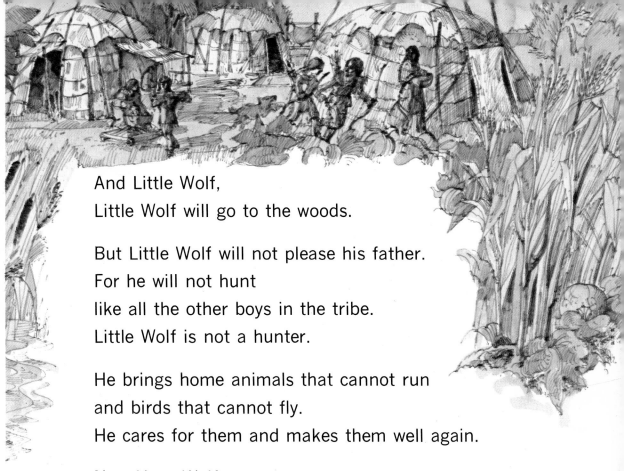

And Little Wolf,
Little Wolf will go to the woods.

But Little Wolf will not please his father.
For he will not hunt
like all the other boys in the tribe.
Little Wolf is not a hunter.

He brings home animals that cannot run
and birds that cannot fly.
He cares for them and makes them well again.

Now Hunt Wolf roars
like the angry thunder god.
"Today, you will hunt!"
he commands Little Wolf.
Little Wolf looks up at his father.

"You are brave," his father says.
"I have seen you wrestle with Big Knife.
But what good is your bravery if you do not
face the sharp antlers of the deer?

"You are swift.
I have seen you race Fast-as-the-Wind.
But what good is your swiftness
if you do not follow the fleeing rabbit?

"You are wise.
You know when rain will fall
and where the big fish swim.
But what good is your wisdom
if you do not trick the sly fox?

"You are brave. And swift. And wise.
You are all these things.
But all these things are nothing
if you do not hunt!"

Now Wise Wolf speaks.
"I know we must kill animals," he says.
"Our people would die if we did not hunt for food.
But let the boy be.
There are other ways."

Hunt Wolf shakes his head.
"No! My son shames me."

"Go now!" he tells Little Wolf.
"And come home when you have killed a deer
or a rabbit or a fox."

So Little Wolf takes his bow and arrow
and leaves his house.
He walks by the houses of all the hunters.
He walks by the Chief's house.
He sees the Chief's only son, Brave Bear.
Brave Bear is very small,
but he is going to be a mighty hunter.

Little Wolf greets the Chief and his son.
But they do not speak to him,
for Little Wolf is not a hunter
like all the other boys in the tribe.

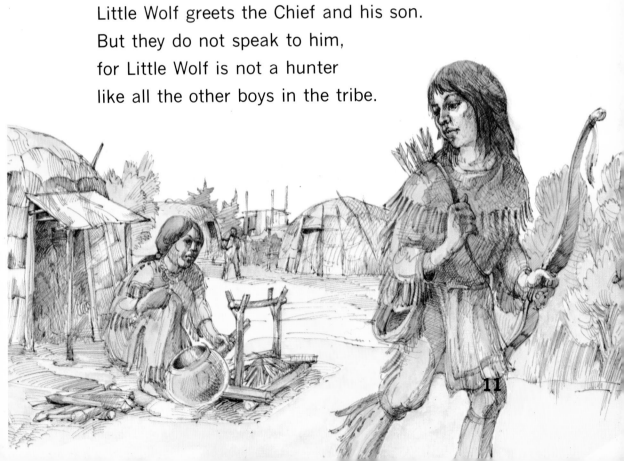

11

Little Wolf goes to the woods.
Everything is very green.
Everything is very quiet.

He knows the woods well.
Wise Wolf has taught him the ways of the woods.
He has taught him about the animals
and about the plants that grow
in the green, quiet woods.
Plants that make men sick,
and plants that make men well.

Soon Little Wolf sees two big brown eyes.
The big brown eyes of a deer.
Little Wolf throws down his bow and arrow.
"How can I be a hunter?" he asks softly.
"How can I be a hunter, if I have to kill you?"

The deer is dark brown velvet running deep
into the woods.

Then Little Wolf sees a round white tail.
The round white tail of a rabbit.
"I will not be a hunter," he says softly.
"I will not be a hunter if I have to kill you."

The rabbit is a quick quiver in the grass,
and is gone.

Then Little Wolf sees a long nose.
The long nose of a fox.
"Never, never will I hunt," he says.
"Never, never will I hunt if I have to kill you."
Then Little Wolf sees the tail of the fox.
It is caught in a trap.
Little Wolf opens the trap and sets the fox free.

The fox is a bounding blur of bright copper.

Now it is night. The moon begins to rise.
The moon rises higher and higher in the sky.
It shines on all the houses of the Indian tribe.

The moon shines on the mother—Flower Wolf.
And on the father—Hunt Wolf.
And on the old grandfather—Wise Wolf.

And on the boy—Little Wolf.

Little Wolf is leaving the woods.
The dark quiet woods.
The trees standing close to the moon.
The plants sleeping near to the earth.

Little Wolf has nothing to show his father.
No deer. No rabbit. No fox.
But he is going home.

Then, in the dark quiet night, he hears a cry.
Little Wolf moves quickly, quietly.
He follows the sound of the cry.

There, under the giant oak,
lies Brave Bear, the Chief's only son.

Brave Bear cries out, "I am dying.
The pain is like a hundred arrows
shooting through me."

Little Wolf sees some berries lying near.
He knows these are berries that make men sick.
He knows Brave Bear has eaten the berries.

"Run for help," Brave Bear moans.
"Run for my father—hurry!"

"I can help you," Little Wolf says.
"You?" Brave Bear says.
"What can *you* do? My father says
you cannot even hunt!"

Little Wolf says, "I know the secrets
of the woods.
I can help you."

Little Wolf leaves Brave Bear.
Soon, he returns with grasses and herbs.

"Eat these," Little Wolf says,
"and you will be well
when the sun shines again."

All night, Little Wolf stays with Brave Bear.
The two boys sleep in the woods.
In the moon-filled quiet woods.

16

Now it is the morning of the next day.
The sun begins to rise.
The sun rises higher and higher in the sky.
The sun shines on the two boys
who are going home.

Brave Bear goes home with Little Wolf.
He tells Hunt Wolf and Flower Wolf and
Wise Wolf what has happened in the woods.

Hunt Wolf says,
"I am glad you are well, Brave Bear.
Our tribe needs you.
You will be a mighty hunter some day."

Then Hunt Wolf looks at his son and smiles.
"Our tribe needs you, too, Little Wolf.
You will be a mighty healer some day."
And Wise Wolf nods his head.

This day Flower Wolf will cook.
Hunt Wolf will hunt.
Wise Wolf will sit by the fire.
And Little Wolf,
Little Wolf will go to the woods.

He will not kill the deer or the rabbit or the fox.
He will see the animals
that run through the woods.
He will watch them.
And he will learn.

He will see the plants that grow in the woods.
He will study them.
And he will learn.

And that is Little Wolf's way.

Ann McGovern

Robert, Who Is Often a Stranger to Himself

Do you ever look in the looking-glass
And see a stranger there?
A child you know and do not know,
Wearing what you wear?

Gwendolyn Brooks

Lonely Maria

Maria lived with her family on a small island in the West Indies. Her father was a fisherman. Every day he went out in his boat with his fish traps. Her mother was busy doing work near their house.

At night as Maria lay in bed she could hear the leaves rustling as though they were whispering together, but she could never understand what they said.

Maria's grandfather was an old man.

Every fine day he sat outside their house, sometimes in the sun, sometimes in the shade. He was always busy making or mending fish nets.

No other children lived near Maria. The sea was her best friend.

It talked with Maria, and at night it sang her to sleep. It sent its waves along the shore to play games with her. It brought her gifts of shells. And it gave her the sandy beach all for her own.

Maria loved the beach. She often sat there and drew pictures in the sand with a stick. She was like her grandfather. She could make things with her hands.

But one day she grew tired of all her games.

She went to her grandfather.

"Grandfather," she said, "I am lonely."

Her grandfather sat and for a long time he looked out across the sea.

Then he said, "I, too, used to be lonely when I went fishing all alone in my boat. But at last I learned that I could make anything happen. I remember how one day my little boat was surrounded by mermaids, all playing music."

"How did you do it, Grandfather?" Maria asked.

"Everyone must find her own way," said her grandfather.

So Maria went back to her beach and thought and thought and thought, and at last she picked up a stick and drew a picture of a house in the sand.

Thinking of the house, Maria closed her eyes, and when she opened them, a wonderful thing had happened. There stood the house and she could go into it whenever she liked.

Now the next day, Maria thought that she would like a garden, so she took her stick and drew flowers in the sand. And when she had closed her eyes, up sprang all sorts of beautiful flowers, filling the air with their sweetness.

But when Maria's father came back from his fishing, he walked past her new house and right through her garden and never saw them.

The very next morning, Maria drew a goat in the sand. No sooner had she closed and opened her eyes than the goat bleated. She was as white as the foam of the sea, so Maria named her Blanca.

Now came a day when the wind began to blow and clouds appeared over the sea. Maria knew that a storm would come soon. Quickly she took her stick and drew a horse in the sand, and when she opened her eyes, the horse neighed. He was gray and white like the clouds over the sea, and Maria named him Pinto.

Then Maria climbed on Pinto's back and with Blanca following, she raced across the island. She raced right past her own house, but neither her mother at the window, nor her grandfather mending nets by the open door, saw her go by.

The next day the sea was fierce and Maria's
father did not go fishing. When Maria put a shawl
over her head to go out, her mother said, "It is
too windy, Maria."

"I will be gone only a little tiny minute,"
promised Maria.

The waves and wind were very noisy, but Maria,
holding tight to the blowing shawl, ran down to
see her house and garden and Blanca and Pinto.

"Be careful of them," she said to the waves,
and ran back to her house fast, fast, with the
wind behind her.

Soon after, came the rain.

All that day the wind and rain howled across the island, tearing at the palm leaf roof of the house. Fiercely the waves threw themselves far up the shores. But early next morning, when Maria woke, the storm was over and the sun was shining again.

Maria crept out of the house on tiptoe so as not to disturb the others.

But when Maria came to the beach, she found no house, no garden, no Blanca, no Pinto! The storm had washed them all away.

Maria thought that her heart would break. For a long, long time she ran up and down the beach looking and calling for her lost friends. But at last Maria knew that it was no use. The sea had taken them away.

What should she do? Maria turned to go home. But no. That would not help. She came slowly back to the beach. The storm had uprooted a tree. Maria sat down on the smooth trunk and thought and thought.

For a long time she sat there, looking out at the sea.

Then suddenly Maria jumped up. She had made up her mind what to do. Only Maria could help Maria now. She ran along the beach until she found a stick. Then she drew something very fast in the sand. She was frowning. Once or twice she rubbed out what she had drawn with one foot, and drew it over again.

When Maria had finished, she stood looking at her picture and shook her head. She added something and looked again. Then at last she gave a little nod. It would have to do.

Maria closed her eyes, and when she opened them what in the wide world do you suppose she saw standing there on the beach, very large and very gentle?

It was an elephant!

Perhaps the elephant wasn't quite like other elephants. Maria had seen a picture of an elephant named Jumbo in one of her mother's old school books, but she had not looked at it carefully.

Still, he was very large and grand. And he was an elephant. From the moment she laid eyes on him, Maria loved him. She named him Jumbo.

Jumbo knew how to act like an elephant. He knelt down and with his trunk lifted Maria and put her on his head.

From her high seat Maria looked down at her great friend, the sea, and smiled.

"You can take everything away from me, if you want to. I'll be unhappy but I'll start right over again," she said. "If you take Jumbo, I'll make a giraffe with a red saddle, and if someday you take my giraffe, I'll," she stopped to think of the most wonderful creature she could think of, and then said, all in a rush, "I'll make a gentle dragon and ride *it!* I'll always be able to make *something* wonderful, whatever you do!"

30

And calling goodbye to the sea, Maria rode off, while all the waves stood on tiptoe to watch her go and waved their white caps gaily.

Elizabeth Coatsworth

Fidelia

Fidelia Ortega belonged to a musical family. Fidelia's brother and sister played in the school orchestra. Alberto played the trombone, and Carmela played the clarinet.

The orchestra played for assemblies and P.T.A. meetings, and once a year the best players were chosen to be in the All City Orchestra.

Fidelia didn't play anything. She wanted, more than anything, to play in the school orchestra. She wanted to play a shiny brown violin.

"But you can't," said Alberto. "Your arms are too short. Your hands are too small. You could not draw the bow. You could not hold the strings down tight."

"You are too young," said Carmela.

Fidelia thought, I will talk to Miss Toomey, the music teacher.

She stopped by the music room and peeked around the door. The orchestra was practicing.

Fidelia crept through the door. A lovely shiver tiptoed up her spine as the violins sang pure and sweet.

Fidelia pretended she was playing a violin. She closed her eyes and took a step closer.

Crash! Bang! Fidelia stumbled right into the percussion section. Timpani and snare drums bounced. Cymbals flew. The xylophone clattered.

Miss Toomey lowered her baton. Everybody
stopped playing and looked at Fidelia.

"What have we here?" asked Miss Toomey.

"It's our sister Fidelia," explained Carmela.
"She wants to play in the orchestra."

"What do you want to play?" asked Miss Toomey.

"Violin," whispered Fidelia.

"You are a bit young to be a violinist. The violin is a difficult instrument. However, we need another drummer. Would you like to try?" asked Miss Toomey.

"Yes," said Fidelia.

So Fidelia played the drum with the orchestra. It was fun, but it wasn't the same as singing out the melody on a beautiful violin. Still, Fidelia did her best.

One morning at orchestra practice Miss Toomey said, "Boys and girls, the time has come to choose the players for the All City Orchestra. Mrs. Reed, the orchestra supervisor, is coming next week. She will listen to you play and decide who will represent our school."

Everybody began to talk at once. All the children wanted to play their best piece for Mrs. Reed.

Tap! Tap! Tap! Miss Toomey's baton called for order.

They began to practice again. Fidelia beat her drum with a heavy heart. What could she play for Mrs. Reed? If only she had a violin.

Then Fidelia had an idea. On her way home from school, she stopped by the store to get an empty cigar box.

Then she stopped by a new building that was going up. Fidelia poked into the pile of scrap lumber at the curb. At last she found a narrow board that looked about right.

At home Fidelia worked very hard. With the cigar box, the board, some nails, and rubber bands, Fidelia made her own violin.

After nailing four nails at each end of the board on the cigar box, Fidelia stretched rubber bands across the board.

Twang, bzzz, thwank, she plucked.

"It sounds awful! I need a bridge for the strings to go over. Maybe then it will sound better. I'll make the rubber bands tighter too."

Fidelia slid a clothespin under the rubber bands, then she picked up her violin and tried again.

"It still sounds like rubber bands," she thought, "but it is better than it was."

So Fidelia placed the violin carefully under her jaw and plucked away with her right hand while she pressed down on the rubber-band strings with the fingers of her left hand. She began to practice.

By evening the ends of Fidelia's fingers were sore. But she knew exactly how to make the sounds she wanted.

The day came for Mrs. Reed to choose the players for the All City Orchestra. Fidelia wrapped her violin in a piece of old sheet and put it in a shopping bag.

The orchestra was tuning up when Fidelia tiptoed through the door. She put her shopping bag in the corner and got the drum.

She watched Miss Toomey. She counted carefully. She played her very best. And all the while she thought her heart must sound louder than the drum.

After the orchestra finished, Mrs. Reed clapped.

Miss Toomey said, "Next, we will play 'Lullaby.'"

That was what Fidelia had been waiting for. Quietly, she unwrapped the cigar-box violin and tucked it under her jaw.

The silvery little melody of the solo violins slipped around the room like moonlight. Fidelia knew just where to place her fingers to match the notes.

Bzzz . . . bzzz . . . zubb . . . zubb . . . !

Miss Toomey tapped her baton on her music stand.

Bzzz . . . bz . . . . Suddenly Fidelia saw that everyone else had stopped playing. They were all looking at her.

"Fidelia, what is that?" asked Miss Toomey.

"It's my own violin. I made it."

Mrs. Reed held out her hand. "May I see it?" she asked. She examined the cigar-box violin.

"It was a good idea. But I'm afraid you cannot play a tune on this violin. Only pretend music."

"Oh, but I can play a tune," said Fidelia. "I practiced. I will show you."

Fidelia tucked the cigar-box violin under her jaw and began to pluck away at the rubber bands.

Sure enough, a good listener could hear the tune of "The Farmer in the Dell" among the twanging, buzzing rubber-band noises.

Mrs. Reed was a good listener. She watched closely, too. "Where did you learn the correct position for playing a violin?" she asked when Fidelia had finished.

"I watched the others. I did what I heard Miss Toomey tell them to do."

"Would you like to play a real violin?"

"Oh, yes!" said Fidelia.

"Hm," said Mrs. Reed. She took Miss Toomey aside and spoke to her softly. Miss Toomey smiled and called to Alberto.

Mrs. Reed handed Alberto her car keys and whispered in his ear. Alberto ran out the door. In two minutes he was back. Under his arm was the smallest violin case any of the children had ever seen.

Mrs. Reed opened the case. "This is a quarter-size violin, boys and girls. Let's see how it fits Fidelia."

It fit Fidelia exactly right.

"Fidelia," said Mrs. Reed, "the boy who was using this violin has grown into a larger size, so I am going to leave it here for you to use. Miss Toomey will start you in beginning string class. I will come back in a month to see how you are getting along."

"Wonderful!" exclaimed Fidelia.

Mrs. Reed laughed. "If you do as well as I think you will, I'm sure you will be in the All City Orchestra next year."

The musical family of Fidelia Ortega was well represented in the All City Orchestra.

Alberto played the trombone and Carmela played the clarinet.

This year it was Fidelia's turn to sit in the audience and clap. But she didn't care. She had a violin exactly her size and she was in the beginning string class.

Everybody has to start somewhere.

Ruth Adams

Lemons and Apples

One day I might feel
Mean,
And squinched up inside,
Like a mouth sucking on a
Lemon.

The next day I could
Feel
Whole and happy
And right,
Like an unbitten apple.

Mary Neville

45

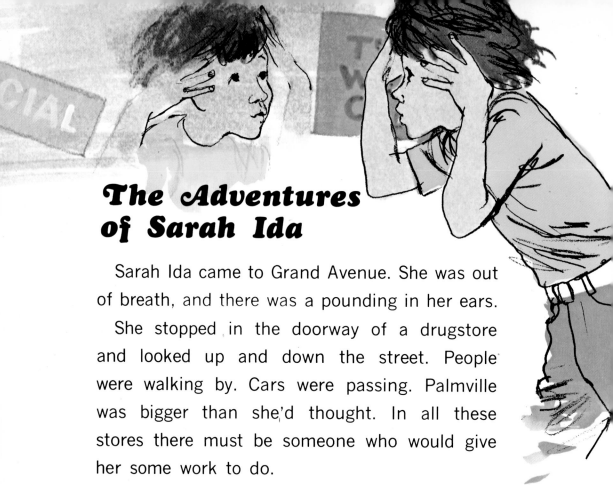

The Adventures of Sarah Ida

Sarah Ida came to Grand Avenue. She was out of breath, and there was a pounding in her ears.

She stopped in the doorway of a drugstore and looked up and down the street. People were walking by. Cars were passing. Palmville was bigger than she'd thought. In all these stores there must be someone who would give her some work to do.

There was a dress shop across the street, with girls' dresses in the window. She might try there. But she wasn't even wearing a dress, and she didn't look very neat.

She used the drugstore window as a mirror and tried to brush back her hair with her hands. Inside the store a woman was watching her. She looked friendly. Sarah Ida went in.

"Can I help you?" asked the woman.

46

"I—" Sarah Ida began, and she couldn't go on. How could she say "I want to work for you"? What kind of work could she do in a drugstore?

"Yes?" said the woman.

"I'm just looking," said Sarah Ida. She looked at the candy. But she couldn't say, "I'll have this and this," because she didn't have any money.

She went outside. She walked past a bank and a hardware store. She came to a pet shop. There were puppies in one window and kittens in the other. She put out her hand to the puppies. One of them came to the window and put his nose against the glass.

She went into the shop. A man and woman were there. All about the shop were animals in cages. There were birds, and in one cage was a green and yellow parrot.

"Do you need help here?" asked Sarah Ida.

The parrot began to squawk. "Polly, Polly! Pretty Polly! My, oh my!"

"What?" asked the woman.

"I said, do you need help!" shouted Sarah Ida.

The woman threw a cloth over the cage, and the parrot was quiet.

"Now. What was it you wanted?" she asked.

"I wanted to work for you," said Sarah Ida.

"Oh," said the woman.

The man spoke. "What do you know about animals?"

"Not much, but I could learn."

The man said, "Come back when you're a little older."

"How much older?"

"About six years," said the man.

"Do you know where I *could* get work?" she asked.

"What can you do?"

"I—I don't know."

"You might try Al," said the man. "He's got a sign up."

"Yes," said the woman. "He's had it up for a long time."

"He's on the corner." The man pointed.

"Why don't you have a look?"

Sarah Ida left the shop. She was sure the man and woman had just been trying to get rid of her. She thought they might be laughing at her, too.

She went on down the street. And there on the corner she saw the sign. It wasn't very big, and it was stuck to a folding door. It said "Help Wanted."

The folding door was at one end of a shoeshine stand. The stand was a kind of shed with a platform in it. There were four chairs on the platform. Above the chairs was a big sign: "Al's Shoeshine Corner."

A man sat on one of the chairs. His face was hidden behind the newspaper he was reading.

Sarah Ida looked at the "Help Wanted" sign. She looked at the stand. This was the place, she thought. This was just the place!

She would tell Aunt Claudia, "I have a job."

"What kind?" Aunt Claudia would ask.

"Working at a shoeshine stand," Sarah Ida would say. "A shoeshine stand on Grand Avenue."

"Oh, you can't do that!" Aunt Claudia would say.

"You said you wouldn't keep me from earning some money," Sarah Ida would say.

"But you can't be seen working at a shoeshine stand on Grand Avenue," Aunt Claudia would say. "I'll *give* you some money!"

Sarah Ida spoke to the man. "Are you Al?"

He put down the newspaper, and she saw his face. He was not young. His hair was thin and gray. His eyes looked like little pieces of coal set far back in his head.

"Yes, I'm Al." He slid down off the chair. His shoulders were stooped. He wasn't much taller than she was. "Do you want something?"

"I'm Sarah Ida Becker," she said, "and I want to work for you."

"What do you mean, work for me?"

"Your sign says 'Help Wanted.' "

"I put that up so long ago I forgot about it," he said. "No one wants to work for me. People don't like to get their hands dirty. They want to do something easy that pays big money."

"Will you give me a job?" Sarah Ida asked.

"You're not a boy."

"The sign doesn't say you wanted a boy."

A man came by.

"Shine?" asked Al.

The man climbed into a chair. Al shined his shoes. The man paid Al and went on.

Al looked at Sarah Ida. "Are you still here?"

"If I worked for you, what would I have to do?" she asked.

"Shine shoes, same as I do. Some days I get more work than I can take care of. Then I need help. But whoever heard of a shoeshine girl?"

"Why couldn't a girl shine shoes?"

"Why don't you go on home?"

"You said you needed help. You've got your sign up."

AL'S SHOESHINE CORNER

51

"What do you want to work here for?"

"I need some money."

"You wouldn't get rich here."

"I know that."

He looked her up and down. "I don't think you really want to work."

All at once she was tired of waiting, tired of talking. She started away.

Al said, "What did you say your name was? Sarah what?"

"Sarah Ida Becker."

"Are you related to the woman that used to be in the library? Are you related to Claudia Becker?"

"She's my aunt."

Another man stopped for a shoeshine. When he was gone, Al asked her, "Do you live with your aunt?"

"Yes," she said.

"Go tell her you saw Al Winkler. Tell her you want to work for me. Maybe—"

"Maybe what?"

"I don't know yet," he said. "First you see what she says."

Aunt Claudia was waiting on the porch. "Where have you been?" she asked, when Sarah Ida came up the steps.

"On the avenue."

"What were you doing?"

"Looking for a job. And I found one."

"You found one?"

"Yes, I did."

"Where?"

"On Grand Avenue. Working for the shoeshine man."

"*Who?*"

"Al Winkler, the shoeshine man."

Aunt Claudia looked dazed. "How did you know him?"

"I didn't know him. He had a 'Help Wanted' sign and I stopped."

"Al Winkler," said Aunt Claudia, as if she were talking to herself. "I remember him so well. He came to the library when I worked there. Does he want you to work at his stand?"

"He said to talk to you about it."

"Do you want to work for him?" asked Aunt Claudia.

"I told you, I want some money of my own."

"This might be a good way to earn some," said Aunt Claudia.

"You *want* me to shine shoes on Grand Avenue?"

"If that's what you want to do."

Sarah Ida was quiet for a while. Things weren't working out the way she'd planned. She'd never thought Aunt Claudia would let her work in the shoeshine stand, and Aunt Claudia didn't seem to care!

But—Sarah Ida had another thought. Maybe Aunt Claudia didn't believe she'd go through with it. Maybe she was thinking, *That child is playing another game.*

Sarah Ida said, "You really want me to go tell Al Winkler I'll work for him?"

"If it's what you want to do," said Aunt Claudia.

Sarah Ida started down the steps. Aunt Claudia didn't call her back. There was nothing for her to do but go.

She found Al sitting in one of his chairs.

"What did she say?" he asked.

"She said yes."

"Do you want to start now?"

"I don't care," she said.

He opened a drawer under the platform and took out an old piece of cloth. "Use this for an apron. Tie it around you."

She tied it around her waist.

A man stopped at the stand. He was a big man with a round face and a black beard. He climbed into a chair and put his feet on the shoe rests.

"How are you, Mr. Naylor?" said Al.

"Not bad," said the man. "Who's this?"

"This is Sarah Ida, she's helping me," said Al. "She needs practice. Do you mind if she practices on you?"

"I don't mind," said Mr. Naylor.

Al said to Sarah Ida, "I'm going to shine one shoe. You watch what I do. Then you shine the other one."

He took two soft brushes and brushed the man's shoe.

"That takes off the dust," he said. "Always start with a clean shoe."

He picked up a jar of water with an old toothbrush in it. With the toothbrush he sprinkled a few drops of water on the shoe.

"That makes a better shine." He opened a round can of brown polish. With his fingers he spread polish on the shoe.

"Now you lay your cloth over the shoe," he
said. "Stretch it tight—like this. Pull it back and
forth—like this. Rub it hard and fast. First the
toe—then the sides—then the back."

When he put down the cloth, the shoe shone
like glass. He untied the man's shoelace. He
drew it a little tighter and tied it again.

He asked Sarah Ida, "Did you see everything
I did?"

"Yes," she said.

"All right. Let's see you do it."

She picked up the brushes. She dropped one.
When she bent to pick it up, she dropped the
other one. Her face grew hot.

She brushed the shoe. She sprinkled the water.

"Not so much," Al told her. "You don't need much."

She looked at the brown polish. "Do I have to get this on my fingers?"

"You can put it on with a rag, but it's not the best way. You can rub it in better with your fingers."

"I don't want to get it on my hands."

"Your hands will wash."

She put the polish on with her fingers. She shined Mr. Naylor's shoe. She untied his shoelace, pulled it tight, and tried to tie it again.

Al tied it for her. "It's hard to tie someone else's shoe when you've never done it before."

Mr. Naylor looked at his shoes. "Best shine I've had all year," he said. He paid Al. He gave Sarah Ida a dollar bill.

After he had gone, she asked Al, "Why did he give me this?"

"That's your tip," said Al. "You didn't earn it. He gave it to you because you're just getting started."

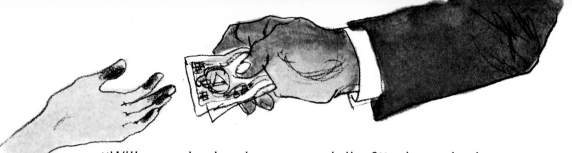

"Will everybody give me a dollar?" she asked.

"No," he said, "and don't be looking for it."

Others stopped at the stand. Sometimes two or three were there at once. Part of the time Sarah Ida put polish on shoes. Part of the time she used the polishing cloth.

Toward the end of the day she grew tired. She tried to hurry. That was when she put black polish on a man's brown shoe.

The man began to shout. "Look what you did!"

"It's not hurt," said Al. "I can take the black polish off. Sarah Ida, hand me the jar of water."

She reached for the jar and knocked it over. All the water ran out.

"Go around the corner to the filling station," Al told her. "There's a drinking fountain outside. Fill the jar and bring it back."

Sarah Ida brought the water. Al washed the man's shoe. All the black polish came off.

"See?" he said. "It's as good as new."

"Well, maybe," said the man, "but I don't want her giving me any more shines."

He went away.

Sarah Ida made a face. "He was mean."

"No, he wasn't," said Al. "He just didn't want black polish on his brown shoes."

"Anyone can make a mistake," she said.

"That's right. Just don't make too many." He said, "You can go now." He gave her a dollar. "This is to go with your other dollar."

"Is that all the pay I get?"

"You'll get more when you're worth more," he said. "You can come back tomorrow afternoon. That's my busy time. Come about one."

She turned around and walked away. Sarah Ida had a job.

Clyde Robert Bulla

I Have a Dream

Maria was lonely so she imagined friends who were pretend animals. Little Wolf dreamed of being a helper, not a hunter. Fidelia dreamed of playing violin in the school orchestra. Sarah Ida wanted a job so she could earn some money.

All of these people had goals for themselves. What are your dreams? What would you like to do? Would you like to . . .

. . . race down the street in a fire engine?

. . . help sick people in a hospital?

. . . dive for treasure in the sea?

. . . take cars apart and put them together again?

. . . look at moon rocks in a space capsule?

. . . sing in front of a TV camera?

. . . ride an elephant in the circus?

Think of at least two things you would like to do. Will you tell these dreams to someone, or will you keep them to yourself?

Developing respect for ideas and goals

62

Fancy That

Dooly
and the
Snortsnoot

There was once a family of giants.

The father giant was taller than a two-story building.

The mother giant was that tall too.

And they had a son, named Dooly, who wasn't any bigger than you.

Now, while your size is just right for YOU, it's a bit small for a giant. Dooly's mother and father worried about him.

Mother said, "Eat your vegetables, Dooly, so you'll grow big and strong like me and your father."

But it was plain to see that it was going to take an awful lot of vegetables.

Dooly did as he was told, but nothing seemed to help. He never got any bigger.

"I'll always be little!" said Dooly, and he started to cry.

"Little or big, you're still a giant," Father reminded him. "And giants don't cry. Giants are brave."

It's hard to be brave when you're not very big. But Father was right. Dooly was a giant, whatever his size.

One of the things that giants do is say, "FEE FI FO FUM!" at people and scare them half out of their wits. This makes the giant feel important. And when you feel important, you feel big.

So one day Dooly went into the village to scare somebody.

The first person Dooly saw was a girl named Treena.

Dooly stood on tiptoe to make himself as tall as he could, made a scowly face, and said, "FEE FI FO FUM!"

Treena giggled.

"I'm a GIANT!" Dooly declared.

"Not a very scary one," said Treena. Then, quite suddenly, she shouted, "FEE FI FO FUM!"

Dooly was so startled he jumped a foot.

"THAT'S the way to do it!" said Treena.

Some other children came over to ask what was going on.

"We're being giants," Treena explained.

So all the children, who had been wondering what to play next anyway, went around on their tiptoes saying, "FEE FI FO FUM!" And Dooly had to admit that most of them did it better than he could.

After a while they got tired of being giants and began to play tag. Dooly was "it" most of the time.

Dooly went into the village and played with the other children quite often after that.

He liked being with them, but he wasn't very good at their games.

When they played baseball, he was first one out.

When they ran a race, he was last one in.

And when they played hide-and-go-seek, Dooly was always the first one found.

He did the best he could, though. And it was fun, even if he didn't ever win.

But every once in a while Dooly would remember that he was a giant. And giants like to feel important. So he would say, "FEE FI FO FUM!"

The children would look up from their games and say, "Not bad, Dooly. Keep trying. Who wants to play blindman's buff?"

But Dooly couldn't help being sad.

One day their play was interrupted by an awful snarling and snorting.

From around the corner came the Terrible Snarly Snortsnoot, who eats little children for lunch! It was gnashing its teeth and thrashing its tail and breathing fire! The Snortsnoot was a terrible sight to see.

The children turned and ran, with the Snortsnoot snarling at their heels.

But the Snortsnoot had decided it wanted to have Treena for lunch.

And with two snorts and a snarl the Snortsnoot leaped and caught her.

It licked its lips and got ready to eat her.

"We've got to get Treena!" shouted Dooly.

"How CAN we?" asked the other children, quivering with fear.

Dooly didn't know. He was just as frightened as they were. But he ran toward the Snortsnoot, determined to do the best he could.

He looked at the Snortsnoot's fierce claws and shivered.

He looked at the Snortsnoot's wicked teeth and trembled.

And THEN he took a deep breath and stomped on the monster's tail.

The Snortsnoot gave a bellow and dropped Treena.

The Snortsnoot scowled a terrible scowl and growled a terrible growl as it turned and went after Dooly. One lunch was as good as another. It would eat Dooly instead of Treena.

Dooly started to run. But then he remembered that he was a giant. And giants are brave. Giants don't run from Snortsnoots, no matter how snarly.

So Dooly stopped running and stood still.

The Snortsnoot opened its mouth to gobble Dooly whole.

Then all of a sudden Dooly said, "FEE FI FO FUM!" right in the monster's face. He said it just the way Treena had taught him.

The Snortsnoot was so surprised it forgot to gobble.

Then the Snortsnoot remembered and opened its mouth again to swallow Dooly.

But something strange had happened. Dooly had grown almost a foot taller.

"So much the better," thought the Snortsnoot. "He'll make a bigger lunch for me." And the Snortsnoot opened its mouth wider.

"FEE FI FO FUM!" said Dooly again. And he grew another foot.

The Snortsnoot opened its mouth as wide as it could. But Dooly was growing too fast.

"FEE!" said Dooly and grew three feet.

"FI!" said Dooly and grew four more.

"FO!" said Dooly, and there was no longer any question that Dooly was a giant.

By the time he reached "FUM!" Dooly was so big he could have swallowed the Snortsnoot.

The Snortsnoot, who wasn't feeling very snarly anymore or hungry either, turned and ran and was never heard of again.

Nobody knew for sure what made Dooly grow.

His father said it was because he ate his vegetables, and no doubt that helped.

"I think," said Dooly's mother, "it was because he did a very big thing."

"I think I just grew up because it was time to," said Dooly modestly.

Jack Kent

How the Wife
Took Care of Things

On a lonely farm in the mountains lived a farmer and his wife. They were neither rich nor poor. The pride of their life was a herd of black and white cows.

One day in the late summer, the farmer decided to go down the mountain to the Fair. As he was leaving, he said to his wife, "I may be very late. Can you take care of things?"

"Certainly," said his wife. So the farmer went on his way, and the wife went about taking care of things. She did not mind being alone. She was busy all day. As night drew on, she built the fire and took up her sewing. Suddenly, she was startled to see a man standing in the doorway. He was stout, had straw-colored hair.

"Good evening," said the farmer's wife.

"Where is your husband?" asked the stranger.

"Busy in the barn, but he will be back shortly."

"I will wait," said the stranger.

"Very well," said the wife quietly and went on with her sewing.

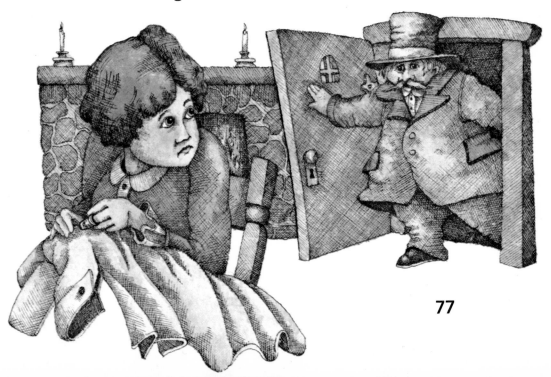

"Your husband thinks he is a great man hereabouts?" asked the stranger, in a voice that showed he thought otherwise.

"Great enough," said the wife. "Are you planning to be a great man, too?"

"I could be, if I wished to," said he.

"Indeed?" said the wife, in a voice that showed she thought otherwise of *that*.

"Indeed," said the stranger, and he suddenly grew until he was ten feet, seven inches tall. His straw-colored hair brushed the roof beam.

If the wife was surprised, she didn't show it. She smiled and said, "Good trick. And yet," she went on thinking wisely, "growing big is easy. Even flowers can grow. But shrinking is another matter. I don't suppose you can shrink?"

"Can I shrink?" cried the stranger in a mean voice. "How about this?" And he shrank to the size of a squirrel. The wife chuckled and picked him up and held him at arm's length.

"Not a bad trick," she agreed. "It would be even better if you could shrink yourself small enough to fit in my thimble but I suppose this is the best you can do."

"We'll see about that," snapped the little man. Then he shrank to the size of a fly. When the farmer's wife saw that, she popped her thimble over him.

"Let me out!" he called in a tiny voice.

"I don't think I'd better do that" said she. "I think I'll wait until my husband comes home. I'll see what he says." So she sat with her thumb held firmly over the thimble's opening and waited. In a while, home came the farmer.

"Did you have a good time at the Fair?" asked his wife.

"Yes," said he, "and I brought you some baskets."

"I have something for you," said she.

"What is it?"

"I have a little man in here."

"How did he get in there?" asked the farmer.

His wife told him all about the stranger. The farmer thought that his wife had been very clever. But he could not for the life of him think what to do with a little man in a thimble.

At last he tapped on the thimble and said, "Sir, are you quite happy in there?"

"No," said the stranger.

"I thought not," said the farmer. "Shall we make a bargain?"

"What sort of bargain?" asked the stranger crossly.

"If I let you out, will you promise to go away and never come near our farm again?"

"No," said the stranger. "As soon as I get out of here, I am going to grow eighteen feet tall. Then we shall see who makes bargains."

"Oh," said the farmer, and, without thinking he began to shake the thimble between his thumb and forefinger. He and his wife thought about what to do next. Very soon the stranger spoke again, sounding very seasick. "Farmer, I have changed my mind. Let me out, and I promise to go away and never come near your farm again."

"And do you promise not to grow until you are far away from here?" asked the wife.

"Yes," said the stranger.

"Good," said the farmer. Then he took the thimble out to the meadow and let the stranger go.

Next morning the farmer and his wife went out to milk their cows. But the animals were nowhere to be seen. The farmer's wife had an idea and hurried out to the meadow. There, under a blackberry bush, she found the whole herd of black and white cows. They were grazing quietly. The largest of them was only three inches high. The smallest cow was no bigger than her thumbnail. She gathered the whole herd in a fold of her skirt and went back to the house.

"I have found the cows," she said. She set the herd on the kitchen table before her startled husband.

"Dear me," said the farmer. "Our wonderful cows! What shall I do with a herd of three-inch cows? That stranger certainly got the best of us!"

The farmer's wife thought for a minute; then she smiled. She whispered something in her husband's ear.

That very day, the farmer and his wife went back down the mountain to show their herd of three-inch cows at the Fair. From near and far, people came to see the remarkable miniature cows—and the farmer and his wife became very rich.

What became of the stranger, I never heard.

Mary Buckley

The Talking Tiger

If a tiger
Walks beside you
And he whispers:
"Where are you going?"
Do not answer,
Just keep walking
Just keep walking, walking, walking.
And if he continues talking
You keep walking.
Let him talk.
You just walk.
A talking tiger
Never bites,
A walking tiger
Never fights.
But if you find
That he's a bore
Then go right home
And shut the door.

Arnold Spilka

84

If You Ever Meet A Whale

If you ever, ever, ever, ever,
   ever meet a whale,
You must never, never, never, never,
   grab it by its tail.
If you ever, ever, ever, ever,
   grab it by its tail—
You will never, never, never, never
   meet another whale!

Traditional Rhyme

How to Tell
the Wild Animals

If ever you should go by chance
    To jungles in the East;
And if there should to you advance
    A large and tawny beast,
If he roars at you as you're dyin'
You'll know it is the Asian Lion.

Or if some time when roaming round,
    A noble wild beast greets you,
With black stripes on a yellow ground,
    Just notice if he eats you.
This simple rule may help you learn
The Bengal Tiger to discern.

86

If strolling forth, a beast you view,
  Whose hide with spots is peppered,
As soon as he has lept on you,
You'll know it is the Leopard.
'Twill do no good to roar with pain,
He'll only lep and lep again.

If when you're walking round your yard,
  You meet a creature there,
Who hugs you very, very hard,
  Be sure it is the Bear.
If you have any doubt, I guess
He'll give you just one more caress.

Carolyn Wells

87

Minnie Maloney & Macaroni

When Minnie Maloney was a small girl, her big sister Molly told her a secret. "If a person buys seven boxes of macaroni each day, it will protect her from bad luck."

When Minnie grew up, she remembered her sister's advice and followed it. But her family never ate macaroni, so she had to give it all away. The macaroni giveaway went on for a long time. Everyone was happy. Everyone except Minnie's husband, Murray.

"This is ridiculous!" he shouted when he saw the grocery bill. "We can't *afford* to buy macaroni that we never eat!"

"Would you like to have bad luck?" was Minnie's reply.

"No," said Murray, heaving a hopeless sigh. And Minnie kept buying macaroni.

Then one day Murray said, "We'll have no more of this nonsense! I don't care if we have bad luck from now until next year! If you don't stop buying macaroni, I will move to Iceland. I'll become a hermit!"

Minnie did not want him to do that, so she promised to stop buying macaroni. But she didn't stop worrying about what might happen. "I just *know* something awful will happen," she said to herself.

Then . . . it happened.

In her nervousness, she tripped on a curb. She broke the heel of her shoe, and dropped her grocery bag. By the time she picked up her groceries and hobbled home, her favorite television program was over.

"Oh, no! This is terrible!" she exclaimed. "What awful thing will happen next?"

Just then Murray came in from the yard. He tripped over the bag of groceries that Minnie had left in the doorway. She put them there while rushing to the television. His glasses fell off and broke.

"This is awful!" he said.

"You see what happens when I don't buy macaroni?" said Minnie.

"Yes," Murray groaned. "I guess your sister is right. You'd better buy some before we have any more bad luck."

The next day Minnie bought seven boxes of macaroni, and everything was fine and dandy.

Then one morning she got a letter from her sister Molly. Molly was planning to come for a visit. Minnie had not seen Molly in a long time. She was very excited when they met at the airport.

The next day Molly went with Minnie to the grocery store. "Why are you buying so much macaroni?" she asked.

"*You* know!" said Minnie.

"No, I don't," said Molly.

"What do you mean? *You're* the one who told me about it!"

"What are you talking about?"

"Don't you remember?" said Minnie. "One day, when we were small, you told me that if a person bought seven boxes of macaroni a day, it would protect her from bad luck.

"Oh, now I remember," said Molly, laughing. "I was only fooling." Then she laughed some more.

Minnie was very angry to find out she had been fooled. She was about to punch Molly in the nose when she got a better idea. After Molly stopped laughing, Minnie paid the grocer for the macaroni.

"You mean you're still going to buy it?" said Molly.

"I sure am," said Minnie. "Maybe you *thought* you were fooling, but it really works."

Later, while her sister took a shower, Minnie told Murray how Molly had fooled them.

"I'll punch her in the nose for that!" shouted Murray.

But when Minnie told him her plan, he changed his mind.

94

After that, strange things began to happen to
Molly. When she got out of the shower, her
shoes were missing. No one could find them.
So, she borrowed a pair from Minnie. The next
day she bought a new pair. But when she got
home, Minnie had found her old shoes. So
Molly returned her new ones to the store. That
night after her shower, her shoes were missing
again.

The next day at breakfast, Murray slipped while serving Molly's orange juice. It spilled all over her dress. Later that day Molly bought some new shoes. But she found her old ones again when she got home. At dinner Minnie slipped while serving the ice cream. It spilled all over Molly's blouse and skirt.

The next day Molly woke up to find both pairs of shoes missing.

"I can't *stand* this!" said Molly. "I've been having so much bad luck! When will it ever stop?"

"Why don't you buy seven boxes of macaroni every day?" said Minnie.

"That's ridiculous!" said Molly.

At breakfast the next day, Murray slipped and spilled pancake syrup on Molly's bathrobe. Molly changed her mind.

97

"I've *had* it!" said Molly. "I'll try *anything!*" With that she walked straight to the grocery. She bought seven boxes of macaroni. Nothing bad happened for the rest of the day.

So Molly bought seven boxes of macaroni every day for the rest of her visit. And she didn't have any more bad luck.

"Thank you so much for telling me about macaroni," she said when they took her to the airport. "I'm going to buy seven boxes every day from now on."

"Don't thank us," said Minnie. "Remember, it was *your* idea."

So they said good-bye, and Molly got on the plane. Then Minnie looked at Murray, and they laughed and laughed.

And they never bought macaroni again.

Mark Stamaty

DRAGON STEW

Once upon a time there was a kingdom ruled by a king who was so fat that his people called him King Chubby. He was so fond of food that he couldn't bear to be without it for very long.

Eating was his hobby. He began with a big breakfast at eight o'clock, had a light snack at ten, and a large lunch at twelve. Then he exercised by watching two tennis players, and since exercise made him hungry, he ate a small snack at about two in the afternoon.

At four, he had sandwiches and at seven in the evening he happily sat down to a royal banquet. There was one of these every evening, even if the king was the only one at the table.

100

Eating was so important to him that it affected everything he did. When he fell in love with a duchess from another kingdom, he told her that he would almost rather look at her than eat a whole roast pig. Needless to say, the duchess never spoke to him again.

His love of eating also got him in trouble in other ways. He was always losing his royal cooks. He just couldn't keep from telling them how to improve their cooking. He insisted on making changes in every dish. Since royal cooks are very proud, they resented this. Six cooks had already left the job.

One evening when the king entered the banquet hall and saw a sandwich on his plate, he knew what had happened.

"Oh, my," he sighed, "I see number seven has left!"

"Yes, your Majesty," replied one of the servants, "he said he could no longer cook for a king who kept changing all his recipes. And now there are no more royal cooks left! None of those you've had will ever come back, and all the others are cooking for other kings. I don't know how to find another cook. There just aren't any!"

The king looked worried for a moment, then brightened. "I know! A royal cook *is* a royal cook because he can make up unusual recipes. We'll have a contest, and the one who tells me the most unusual recipe can be the royal cook!"

The next day signs were put up throughout the kingdom inviting all cooks to enter the contest. There was great excitement. Every cook from every inn in the kingdom came rushing to the castle.

Calling all Cooks!
Notice is hereby given that his royal majesty requires a Royal Cook to tend the royal kitchens and cook the royal meals. He who suggests the most original recipe to the royal personage will get the royal job.

They formed a line which began at the back of the castle, wound around to the front, and crossed the bridge. They entered the gate, jammed the courtyard, went up the stairs, and flowed into the throne room where the king was interviewing them. In they came, bowing, smiling, and offering enough recipes to fill seven fat cookbooks or seventy fat kings.

But to each, King Chubby shook his head. "That's not unusual," he'd say, or "I've had that before."

While this was going on, a shabby young man came trudging up the road toward the castle. He had patched knees and elbows, and the feather in his worn hat was bent, but he had a merry grin, and he was whistling a gay tune. When he saw the long line of people, he asked a soldier, "What's going on?"

"The king's looking for a new royal cook," the soldier replied. "The cook with the most unusual recipe will get the job and will live in the palace off the best of the land!"

"Wouldn't that be wonderful!"

"Well, I don't know," said the soldier. "Cooks don't get along with the king. He tells 'em what to do, puts things in their pots—he all but does the cooking himself."

"You don't say?" said the young man, and he got into line.

"Oh, are you a cook?" asked the soldier.

"I'm just the sort of cook the king wants," he answered, "and I have the most unusual recipe he's ever heard of!"

105

It was late afternoon when he reached the throne room. The king was looking very glum. Not one cook had offered a recipe he thought was unusual. And now the last of them was this shabby fellow who looked far too thin to be much of a cook. "Well, what's your name and recipe?" he asked.

"I'm Klaus Dinkelspiel, your Majesty. My recipe is so unusual, so rare, that I'll bet you've never heard of it. It's—dragon stew!"

The king gasped. "That sounds different. What's in it—besides dragon, of course?"

"Oh, I can't tell you!" said Klaus. "It has been a secret in my family for hundreds of years."

"I understand," nodded the king, "but if we can ever locate a dragon, you must make it for me. However, you can begin preparing a royal banquet for tonight. You are the new royal cook."

Klaus bowed deeply. "And what would you like for dinner?" he asked.

"How about roast pig with applesauce?"

"And would your Majesty care to show me exactly how you want it cooked?" Klaus asked innocently.

The king stared. "You mean you won't care if I offer advice? Why, you and I are going to get along just fine!"

So off they went to the kitchen and got together everything the king needed. Then Klaus said, "Now, how would you prepare this, your Majesty?"

King Chubby, very pleased, stuffed the pig, tied it up, and then peeled and sliced the apples.

"How would you cook this, your Majesty?"

So the king happily popped the pig into the oven. He took turns stirring the applesauce and turning the pig.

Klaus watched and kept saying, "Just how I'd have done it."

When the pig was brown and savory and the sauce bubbling merrily, he said, "I thank you for all your help, sire. If you will go to the banquet hall, I'll serve you the banquet I have prepared."

When the king had gobbled up the last piece of pork and bit of sauce, he announced that it was the finest banquet he'd ever eaten and Klaus was the finest cook he'd ever had. And from then on, the king and his new cook were both pleased—King Chubby because he now had all his favorite dishes cooked exactly as he liked them and Klaus because he was living off the best of the land.

One morning, a good many months after Klaus had become the royal cook, he was called to the throne room. When he entered, he was shocked to see the Captain of the guard and a dozen scratched and smoke-blackened soldiers surrounding a large cage inside of which was a small, fat dragon.

"Surprise!" beamed the king. "I sent them out to find a dragon months ago, and it's taken all this time to find one. Now you can cook your special dragon stew tonight. I promise I won't try to find out your secret—I won't even set foot in the kitchen today!"

The soldiers carried the cage to the kitchen, set it down, and trooped out. The captain said, "Careful of him, Cook—he bites, scratches, and can shoot fire six inches out of his nose."

Klaus stared at the small dragon. A tear rolled down its cheek. "Are you trying to think of the best way to kill me?" it asked. "It isn't fair! I was minding my own business, bothering no one, and suddenly your soldiers attacked me and carried me here to be made into—into stew." He sniffled.

111

"Believe me, dragon," said Klaus, "I don't want to make you into stew. I didn't think there were any dragons when I made up that silly recipe. I just wanted to trick the king into thinking I was a cook. I couldn't make any stew if my life depended on it—and it probably does. The king will have me beheaded when he finds out that I tricked him."

"Oh, making a stew is easy," said the dragon. "You soak the meat in oil and spices, brown it in butter and simmer it slowly in broth with onions and carrots. I always throw in a few mushrooms and some parsley, too. And then . . ."

"You can cook?" interrupted Klaus. "I thought dragons only ate raw princesses and things like that."

"Heavens, no!" the dragon shuddered. "Really, I'm a good cook. Living alone, I've had to do all my own cooking. I've become quite a chef, if I do say so myself." He blew a smoke ring from his left nostril.

Suddenly, Klaus began to grin and nod his head as though he had thought of something.

At seven o'clock, the king hurried into the banquet hall, tingling to taste Klaus' wonderful dragon stew. He watched closely as Klaus carried in a steaming bowl and ladled chunks of beautifully browned meat and vegetables swimming in rich gravy onto the king's plate. King Chubby began to gobble. After four helpings, he leaned back with a sigh.

"That certainly is one of the best stews I've ever eaten. What a shame we can never have it again. That was probably the world's last dragon."

"Oh, we can have it as often as you like, your Majesty," Klaus calmly announced. "You see, the thing that makes dragon stew such a rare recipe is that it can only be cooked *by* a dragon! Allow me to present my assistant."

Klaus whistled, and in came the dragon, wearing a tall, white cook's hat and a gravy-stained apron. He bowed deeply.

"Under my direction," said Klaus with a charming grin, "my assistant will be happy to make dragon stew whenever you want it."

So everything turned out very well. King Chubby was able to cook his own banquets just as he liked them. He could also have dragon stew (made from beef) as often as he wanted it. Klaus was happy to be living off the best of the land without having to work hard for it. The dragon was very pleased to be an assistant royal cook.

But the happiest of all was the kitchen helper. One of his jobs had been to light the fire in the big stove, and he had always burned his knuckles. But now he no longer had this task, for the assistant cook lit his own stove by shooting fire out of his nose!

Tom McGowen

R U O K?

There are certain letters and numbers that sound like words. For example, *8* sounds like *ate* and *c* sounds like *sea*. Can you think of some others?

Try to read the sentences that go with each of the pictures below.

I M N D L-F-8-R

D L-F-N 8 D A

R U O K?
S, N-Q

R U C-P?
S, I M
I M 2

Now try reading some other sentences without the help of any pictures. When you understand each sentence, you might like to draw it.

D C-L S N D C
I C U
E S D 1 4 U 2 C
I M C-N U

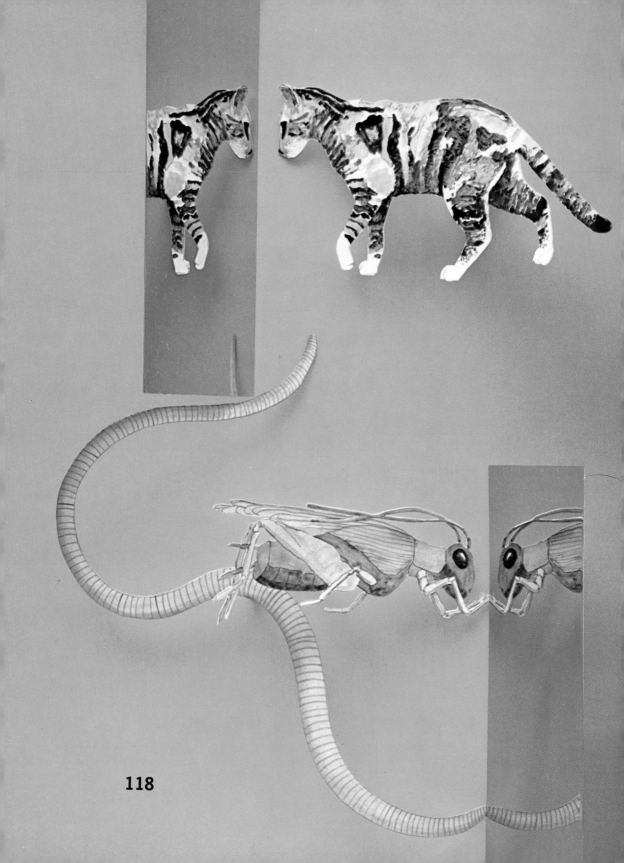

Creature Features

119

What Mary Jo Wanted

Every time Mary Jo saw a dog, any dog—big or little, black, white, old or young—she wished it belonged to her.

"I would rather have a dog than anything on earth," she said at least twice a week, usually at the dinner table. She sighed. "I'd be the happiest person in this town if I had a puppy." She often read the ads from the newspaper under "Pets for Sale" out loud to her parents.

"Puppies must be trained. It takes a lot of time," said her father.

"I'd love to train a puppy!" said Mary Jo. "I'd do it all myself!"

"Puppies cry at night when you first bring them home," said her father. "Nobody gets any sleep."

"They cry because they're lonesome. I'll be the one to get up in the night and talk to my puppy," said Mary Jo.

"They must be fed every day. They must have fresh water. They should be brushed. They must be given baths," said her father.

"I'd do it! I'd do it!" said Mary Jo. "I *want* to feed and brush and wash a dog."

"A good dog owner must take the full responsibility for her pet," said her father.

Responsibility was a word Mary Jo had heard a lot lately—ever since her sister had been given a canary for her birthday. She was being responsible for her bird, but she was quite a bit older than Mary Jo. Besides, a bird in a cage was not as great a responsibility as a puppy.

"I would be responsible," said Mary Jo.

Mary Jo read dog books by the dozen. She drew pictures of dogs. She wrote dog stories and dog poems. One morning she put a two-page theme by her father's plate, "Why I Want a Dog."

It looked as if fate were on Mary Jo's side when a new pet store opened downtown.

She showed the big opening day ad in the newspaper to her parents. She read: "Special for This Opening. Small, lovable puppies. Only $19 while they last!"

"I would like a badger," said Mary Jo's brother. "Do they have any badgers?" Jeff had just been looking at a picture of a badger family in a new book from the library.

"Can't we go down to see the new pet store? And the puppies?" Mary Jo begged.

"All right, Mary Jo. I believe you're old enough to take care of a puppy," said her father.

"Oh," shouted Mary Jo. "Get your coats, everybody! Let's go!"

"They *are* cute," said Mary Jo's mother when they stood gazing down at a little pen full of puppies in the new pet store.

"Cute!" said Mary Jo. "They're the sweetest creatures ever born in this world!"

Her father laughed. "Which one do you want?"

Mary Jo knew right away. One little furry baby had wobbled over to lick her fingers the minute she knelt beside the pen.

"This one," she said. "He came right to me. He's the most lovable!"

"Have him wrapped up then," said her father.

"Wrapped up?" said Mary Jo. Then she saw that her father was joking. He got out his billfold.

The first thing the family did when they got home was to put newspapers all over the kitchen floor.

"It's only until you're housebroken," she told him. He reached playfully for her shoe string and looked up into her face.

"Be sure to call the vet this week and make an appointment," said Mary Jo's father. "He should have his puppy shots right away."

Mary Jo and her friend Laurie spent hours deciding on a name for him. They made lists and pored over the section of names at the back of the dictionary.

Jeff suggested "Mr. Picklepone." That was the silliest name he could think of.

In the end they decided on "Teddy" because the puppy looked so much like a small teddy bear, and he even squeaked.

He squeaked and cried—*especially* at night. No matter how cozy Mary Jo made his bed in the kitchen or how many times Teddy yawned at bedtime, he always woke as soon as everyone was in bed and the house was still. He woke and cried as if his heart would break. Mary Jo put a night-light in the kitchen, in case he was afraid of the dark. She gave him a little snack at bedtime, in case he was hungry. She put an old toy dog in bed with him, hoping he would think it was another puppy. But he didn't.

Mary Jo walked sleepily from her warm bed out to the kitchen a dozen times a night to see Teddy. As long as she was there, he was happy. He tried to get her to play as if it were the middle of the day instead of the middle of the night, and he licked her with his loving puppy tongue. As tired as she was, Mary Jo could never feel angry with him because he was so happy each time she appeared at the kitchen door.

But by the end of the first week she could hardly get up in the mornings. She was almost late for school. Everyone looked tired because although Mary Jo was the one who got up to soothe him, Teddy woke the others with his loud, sad little cries.

A neighbor told them to wrap a clock in a blanket and put that beside Teddy in the bed. "He'll hear the tick and think it's another puppy," she told them. But it didn't fool Teddy for one minute.

Finally one morning Mary Jo's mother found her asleep on the paper covered kitchen floor.

"Is this ever going to end?" Mary Jo's mother asked at the breakfast table. "I don't ever remember hearing of any puppy crying as many nights as this one has."

"Some of them get used to being alone faster than others I guess," said Mary Jo's father. "But I'm beginning to wish we had never seen that dog!"

"I'm responsible," thought Mary Jo. "I've *got* to think of something to keep Teddy quiet."

That afternoon when she went to the basement
to get some old newspapers for the kitchen floor
she saw something that gave her an idea.

After dinner that night Mary Jo said, "You'll
be able to sleep tonight. I've thought of a way to
keep Teddy quiet."

"What is it?" asked her mother.

"You'll see," said Mary Jo. She went down to
the basement.

Her parents heard her lugging something up
the stairs. It was an old folding cot.

"I'm going to sleep in the kitchen until Teddy is housebroken and can sleep in my room," she said.

Her mother and father looked at each other.

"Why not?" said her father. "That's probably the only thing that will solve the problem."

And it did. Teddy slept without making one squeak all night with Mary Jo on the old cot just above his basket.

Mary Jo thought it was fun to sleep in the kitchen. It was cozy to hear the clock hum and the faucet over the sink drip now and then. If she woke at daybreak, it was nice to see the new day arriving in the kitchen so early. There was a window to the east, so sunlight came to the kitchen first.

And it was fun to pretend to be asleep when her mother or father or brother came to the kitchen.

"Mary Jo, wake up!" they would say.

"Oh, is it morning already?" Mary Jo would say. "I was sound asleep."

And she hugged Teddy and tried not to giggle.

Janice May Udry

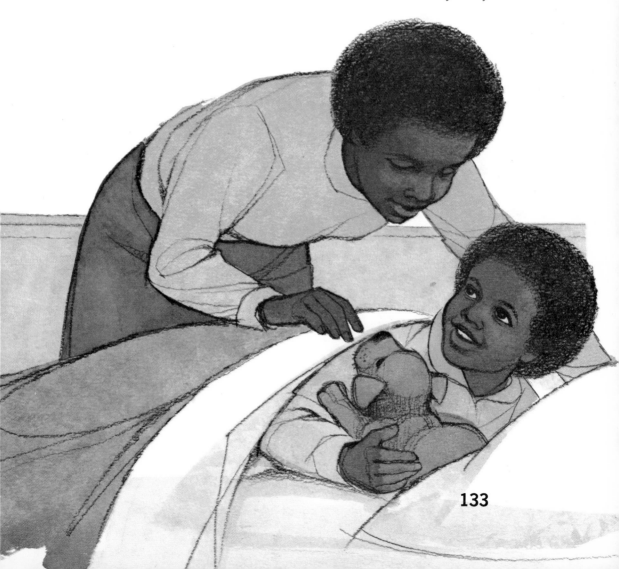

133

CAT

The black cat yawns,
Opens her jaws,
Stretches her legs,
And shows her claws.

Then she gets up
And stands on four
Long stiff legs
And yawns some more.

She shows her sharp teeth,
She stretches her lip,
Her slice of a tongue
Turns up at the tip.

Lifting herself
On her delicate toes,
She arches her back
As high as it goes.

She lets herself down
With particular care,
And pads away
With her tail in the air.

Mary Britton Miller

George

A dog went to live with a family. They did not go out and buy him. And he was not a gift from a friend. They did not find him. He found *them* and he moved in.

He was a big dog. And they were a big family. There was Ma. And Pa. And Grandma. And Grump. There was Alice. And little Anna May. And Willy. They were also a very busy family.

One day Grandma went out fishing in her little boat. And the big dog went along. He was not invited. He just went.

And he leaned too far over the side and the little boat turned over. Grandma lost her fishing rod and her oars and her oarlocks. She lost her bait and her bait box and she had to swim all the way home and she was simply furious.

"This dog must go!" she announced. But the rest of the family was too busy to pay much attention and the dog certainly did not pay any attention at all. Because he liked it there and it was his home.

That evening Grump read in the newspaper that there were to be many special big sales in the stores of a faraway town. The next morning he got up very early and put on his best clothes and jumped into his little car and drove all the many miles to the faraway town. Just when he arrived there and had the little car neatly parked, he heard a snoozing sound and he turned around and there was the big dog asleep on the back seat. He had not been invited. He just went.

Grump could not leave him locked in the car all day and he could not take him into the stores. All he could do was turn around and drive the long way home. He missed all the special big sales and he was simply furious.

"This dog must go!" he demanded. But the rest of the family was too busy to pay much attention and certainly the dog did not pay any attention at all. Because he liked it there and it was his home.

The next day Ma was late in getting ready to go to her office in the city. She had to run and jump onto the very last car of the train just as it was leaving. She hurried to her seat hearing everyone laugh as she went by. She looked down to see if she was still wearing her nightgown or had forgotten to put on her shoes. When she turned around to see if she was wearing her hat backwards she found out why they were laughing. Because there was the big dog paddling along close behind her. He had not been invited. He just went.

The conductor came and pulled the EMERGENCY rope and the train came to an emergency stop. Ma had to get off and walk the dog all the way home. She never did get to work at all that day and she was simply furious.

"This dog must go!" she stamped. But the rest of the family was too busy to pay much attention and the dog certainly did not pay any attention at all. Because he liked it there and it was his home.

The next day Pa invited some very important people to come and visit and stay for tea. And they came. Just when they were all standing on the sea wall looking at the view the big dog ran and leaped over them into the water to chase a clam or possibly a jellyfish or maybe a mermaid, and they all fell in.

Wearing their very best going-to-visit clothes they all fell in. That was the end of the tea party and the important people, and Pa was simply furious.

"This dog must go!" he stomped. But the rest
of the family was too busy to pay much attention
and certainly the dog did not pay any attention
at all. Because he liked it there and it was his
home.

The next day Alice started out on her paper route and the big dog tagged along. He was not invited. He just went.

She rode on her bicycle up one street and down the next, throwing the folded newspapers onto the porches of the houses on her route as she went by.

When she was all finished she rode home with the fine feeling of a hard day's work well done. But when she got there she found that the big dog had picked up all the papers that she had just delivered and carried them home to his own front door. So she had to gather them all up and start in on her paper route all over again and she was simply furious.

"This dog must go!" she steamed. But the rest of the family was too busy to pay much attention and certainly the dog did not pay any attention at all. Because he liked it there and it was his home.

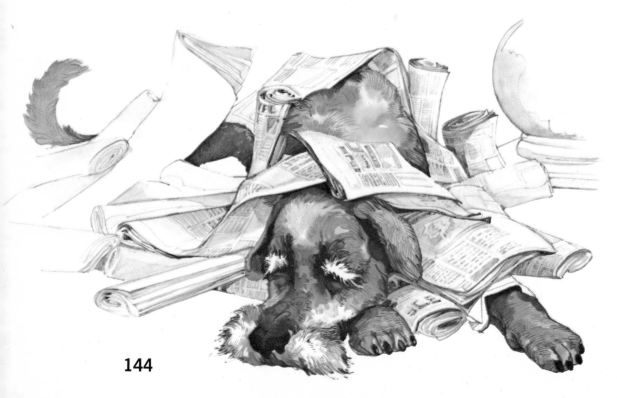

144

The next morning Willy got up early to work in his flower garden. Willy had a beautiful garden. He had worked real hard all the hot summer to help the flowers grow tall and bloom full and bright. He planned to take them to the Fair in hopes that they would earn a prize ribbon there.

But he found that in the night the big dog had dug deep holes and buried big bones right in the middle of his best bed of mums—which is the quick way to say chrysanthemums. The dog had not been invited. He just dug. And now the long strong stems were broken and the little bright buds were squashed and Willy was simply furious.

"This dog must go!" he cried. But the rest of the family was too busy to pay much attention and certainly the dog did not pay any attention at all. Because he liked it there and it was his home.

The next day little Anna May went to the corner store. She took with her all her money that she had been saving for many weeks to buy a baseball and a catcher's mitt. The big dog went along. He was not invited. He just went.

He followed her into the store and there he gobbled up a big box of bonbons and he gobbled up a big box of chocolate cherries. He gobbled up a big box of jelly beans and he gobbled up a big box of gumdrops, and he galloped out of the store bigger than ever. Little Anna May had to use up all her money to pay for what he had eaten. She did not have any left to buy the baseball or the catcher's mitt and she was simply furious.

"This dog must go!" little Anna May sputtered. But the rest of the family was too busy to pay much attention and certainly the big dog did not pay any attention at all. Because he liked it there and it was his home.

And every day the big dog brought home kittens. One by one he carefully carried six kittens home from a neighbor's house because he just loved kittens. And every night the mother cat came to collect her kittens and while she was taking one back to her own home the big dog was bringing another one to *his* home and finally all the mother cat could do was to move in with the dog's family too and she was simply furious.

Also every Saturday he went to the town tennis courts and helped the people there play tennis, but they did not need his kind of help and they were simply furious.

Then on one very hot summer day nothing happened. The big dog did not tag along after anyone. He did not overturn any rowboat. He did not hide in an automobile. He did not climb aboard a railroad train. He did not push any important people into the water. Or any not important people either. He did not bury any bones in any garden. He did not carry home any newspapers. He did not gobble up any jelly beans or gumdrops. He did not carry home kittens or play tennis on the town tennis courts. He did not do anything. Because he was not there. He was gone.

And suddenly the big family felt simply lost without him. They got busy and began to look for him. They called and they whistled and they cried. They telephoned the town dog catcher. And the dog catchers of all the other towns around. They put an ad in the newspaper. They ran up one street and down the next. They rang doorbells and asked for him of everyone they met. They combed the countryside and searched the town. Everyone asked, "What is his name?" And then they were embarrassed when they had to answer that they had been just too busy to give him a name. And now they could not find the big dog anywhere. He was gone.

The neighbors helped in the search. And the people on the tennis court stopped their game and helped to look for him. And also the cat who was the mother of the big dog's kittens. She looked too. But no one could find him. He was gone.

At the end of that very hot day the big busy family gathered together at home to talk things over. They talked over what they had done and what they could do next.

The big dog, hearing their voices, woke from his sound sleep. He crawled out from under the cool back porch, where he had been all day. He yawned and stretched and yawned again. Then he crawled out of the deep cool hole he had dug in the dark earth under the porch.

He walked slowly into the house. They were all astonished to see him. Then they all rushed to greet him. Ma hugged him. And Pa squeezed him. And Grandma patted him. And Grump petted him. Alice cosied him. Little Anna May squoze him. And Willy kissed him. And they gave him a name. They named him George. And they all just love love love loved him.

The big dog did not know what all the fuss was about because he did not know that he had been lost. And the big family did not know he had *not* been lost, so they begged him not to be lost ever again.

The big dog did not understand their words, but of course he did know what they meant. They were saying what they were usually too busy to say. They were saying that they loved him, which of course he had always known. Because that was why he liked it there, and why it was his home.

Phyllis Rowand

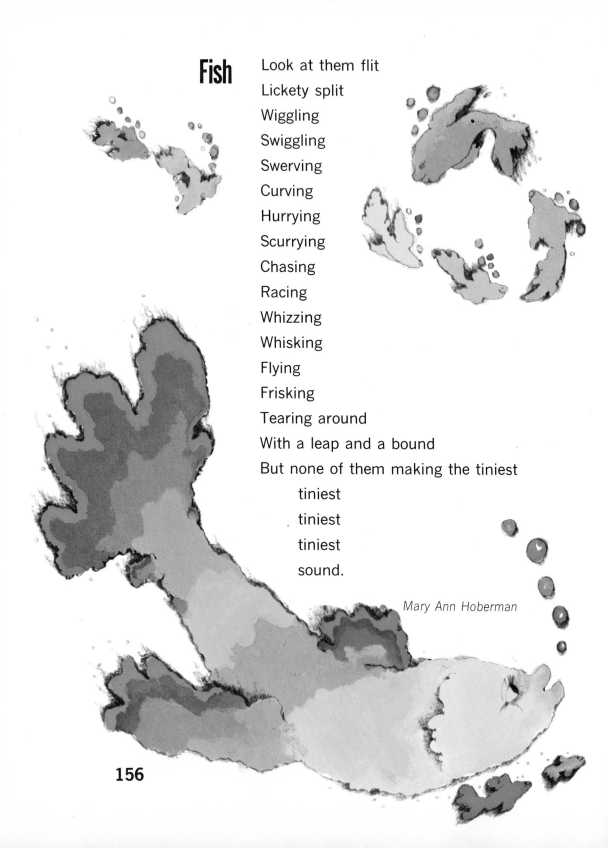

Fish

Look at them flit
Lickety split
Wiggling
Swiggling
Swerving
Curving
Hurrying
Scurrying
Chasing
Racing
Whizzing
Whisking
Flying
Frisking
Tearing around
With a leap and a bound
But none of them making the tiniest
    tiniest
    tiniest
    tiniest
    sound.

Mary Ann Hoberman

156

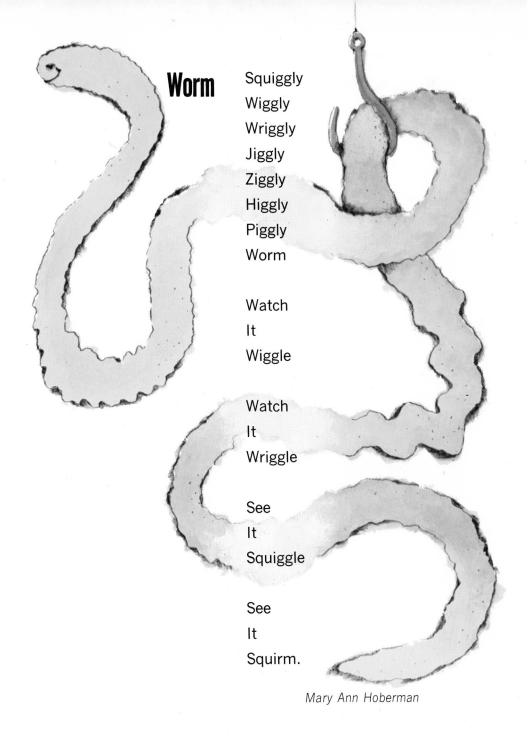

Worm

Squiggly
Wiggly
Wriggly
Jiggly
Ziggly
Higgly
Piggly
Worm

Watch
It
Wiggle

Watch
It
Wriggle

See
It
Squiggle

See
It
Squirm.

Mary Ann Hoberman

157

A Pocketful of Cricket

Part 1

This boy, Jay, lived with his father and his mother in an old farmhouse in a hollow.

All around his house Jay could see hills. He could see hills when he stood in the kitchen doorway. He could see hills when he swung on the gate in front of his house. When he climbed into the apple tree beside his house, he could see hills.

Woods covered most of the hills. Corn grew on some of them. On a far green hill, farther than Jay could see, cows ate grass in a pasture.

Every afternoon, in spring and summer and fall, Jay went to the pasture to drive the cows home.

On this afternoon, late in summer, he set out before sundown, eating a slice of buttered bread.

He walked along the lane on the side of a hill. The dust under his feet felt soft and warm. He spread his toes and watched the dust squirt between them.

After he had walked forward for a while, he turned around and walked backward for a while. As he walked, he looked at his footprints in the dust.

A hickory tree grew beside the lane. Its branches shaded the hillside. Nuts grew among its leaves.

With a stick Jay knocked a nut from a low branch.

He picked up the nut and smelled the tight green hull that enclosed it. The smell tingled in his nose like the smell of the first frost.

Jay put the nut in his pocket.

A creek flowed across the lane at the foot of the hill.

Jay waded into the creek.

The clear water rippling against his ankles cooled his feet. It washed them clean of dust.

Jay wiggled his toes in the smooth brown gravel on the bottom of the creek.

He picked up a small flat rock lying in the water. He turned it over. There was the print of a fern.

Jay put the rock in his pocket.

When Jay waded out of the creek he stood for a minute on the bank.

He watched a crayfish scuttling backward among the rocks.

He watched minnows darting about in the water.

At his feet he saw a gray goose feather. He picked it up, smoothed it with his fingers, and put it in his pocket.

A rail fence zigzagged between the creek and a cornfield.

As Jay walked toward the fence he heard a scratchy noise. He saw a gray lizard slithering along the rail.

He stopped. He stood very still and watched.

The lizard slithered away, out of sight.

Jay climbed the fence. He sat on the top rail.

He heard the wind rustling in the ripening corn.

He heard bugs and beetles ticking.

He heard a cicada fiddling high notes in the summer heat.

He heard an owl hooting in the woods.

Jay climbed down from the fence and walked between two rows of corn.

In the dirt he saw an Indian arrowhead, turned up by a plow. He picked it up, brushed the dirt from it, and put it in his pocket.

Beans had been planted with the corn. The vines climbed the tall cornstalks.

Jay picked a bean pod. With his thumb nail he opened it.

He shelled the beans into his hand. They were white, striped with red speckles. The stripes on every bean were different from the stripes on every other bean.

In Jay's hand the beans felt cool—like morning.

Jay put the beans in his pocket.

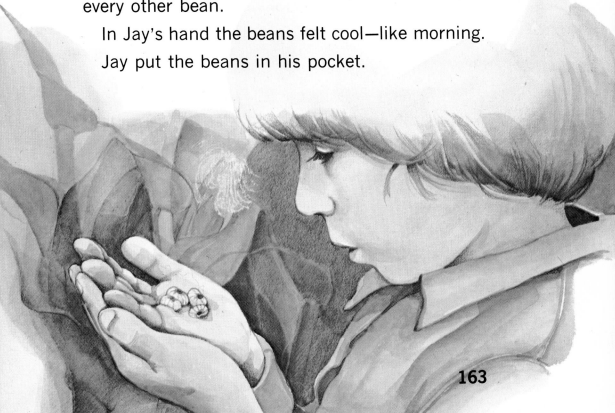

Jay climbed the steep pasture hill where an old apple tree stood. The russet apples that grew on one side of the tree were sweet. The red apples that grew on the other side of the tree were sour.

Jay picked a russet apple with one hand, and a red apple with the other. He took a bite from one apple, then a bite from the other—sweet and sour, sweet and sour.

As he ate, he looked off into the hollow below him. It was long and narrow. A road ran the length of it. At the end of the road stood a white schoolhouse.

Jay looked a long time at the schoolhouse. Then he turned and walked slowly down the hill toward the cows.

The cows looked up from their grazing. They switched their tails and started home. Nodding their heads and switching their tails, they walked, one behind another, along the cow path beside the fence.

Jay walked behind them.

Beside the cow path a cricket jumped.

Jay watched the cricket crawl underneath a stone.

Quietly he lifted an edge of the stone.

Quickly he cupped his hand over the cricket.

He gathered the cricket in both hands. Carrying it gently, he hurried after the cows.

Across the creek he waded.

Along the lane he trudged in the dust.

Into the barn he drove the cows. His father was waiting to milk them.

"What took you so long?" asked Jay's father.

"Nothing," said Jay.

Jay hurried to the house.

"What's that in your hands?" asked Jay's mother.

"Cricket," said Jay.

"What are you going to do with him?" asked Jay's mother.

"Keep him," said Jay.

"What will you do with him when you go to school?" asked Jay's mother.

"How many days till I go to school?" asked Jay.

"Five," said Jay's mother. "Next Monday you'll begin."

"Cricket will stay in my room and wait for me," said Jay.

"You'll need a cage to keep him in," said Jay's mother.

She opened a kitchen drawer and took from it a tea strainer. She tucked the handle of the strainer into Jay's pocket.

Off Jay hurried to his room.

He laid the strainer upside down on his table and put Cricket inside.

He brought Cricket water in a bottle cap.

He brought Cricket a piece of lettuce leaf, a thin slice of cucumber, and a slice of banana.

Cricket sat inside the tea strainer. Jay sat on his bed beside the table and watched.

Cricket sat and Jay sat.

Cricket did not drink the water.

He did not eat the lettuce, nor the cucumber, nor the banana.

"Jay, come to supper!" called Jay's mother.

Jay, on his bed beside the table, watched Cricket.

"Jay!"

After supper Jay hurried back to Cricket.

Some of the lettuce leaf was gone, Jay thought.

A nibble had been nibbled off the cucumber, he thought.

He sat on his bed beside the table and looked at Cricket.

"Do you like your new home, Cricket?" he asked.

Cricket sat and Jay sat.

The light in the room grew dim.

Night came.

Jay pulled the table closer to his bed. He got into bed and fell asleep.

A noise waked him. "Chee! Chee!"

Cricket was fiddling. Cricket was fiddling loud and clear. "Chee! Chee! Chee!"

Jay sat up in bed and listened.

"You do like your new home, don't you, Cricket?" he asked.

"Chee! Chee! Chee!" fiddled Cricket.

Jay reached under his pillow and found his flashlight.

He turned the flashlight on. The fiddling stopped.

Jay turned the flashlight off and put it under his pillow.

He lay down again. In the dark he waited, listening . . . listening.

"Chee! Chee! Chee!" fiddled Cricket.

The next day Jay made Cricket a cage out of a piece of wire screen. It was bigger than the tea strainer.

Every morning Jay brought Cricket fresh pieces of lettuce and cucumber and banana. He put fresh water in the bottle cap.

Every afternoon Jay shut the door of his room, turned Cricket out of his cage, and played with him.

Cricket jumped about the room. Jay jumped after him.

Cricket crawled up the curtain at Jay's window. He jumped to the door of Jay's closet.

"Don't let Cricket in that closet," said Jay's mother. "He might eat your new sweater. Then what would you wear to school?"

Every night, when Jay got into bed and the dark room grew still, Cricket fiddled.

"Chee! Chee! Chee!" And "Chee! Chee! Chee!"

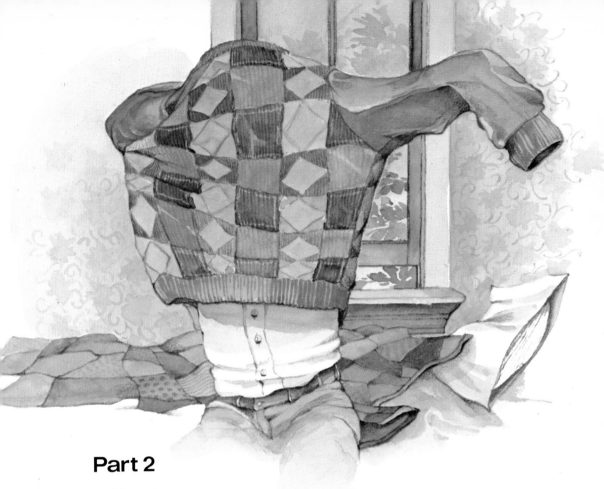

Part 2

Monday came.

Jay was ready for school early.

He said good-bye to Cricket. He looked at Cricket a long time.

"You'd better be going now," said Jay's mother. "You mustn't be late for the bus."

Jay said good-bye to his mother. He said good-bye again to Cricket. He started down the road.

When he had gone a few steps he turned and hurried back. He went into his room. He stood looking at Cricket.

"Jay!" called his mother.

Quickly Jay emptied his pocket. He piled on the table an Indian arrowhead, hickory nuts, buckeyes, and beans.

"Jay!"

Into his pocket Jay tucked Cricket. Away he ran down the road.

At the mailbox Jay waited.

Along came the yellow school bus. It stopped, and the driver opened the door. Jay climbed in. He sat down beside a window in the front of the bus.

The bus was filled with boys and girls. They talked and laughed.

"Chee! Chee!"

Inside Jay's dark pocket Cricket began fiddling.

The talking stopped. Everybody listened.

"Chee! Chee! Chee!" fiddled Cricket.

Jay cupped his hand against his pocket to quiet Cricket.

"Maybe somebody's taking a cricket to Teacher," said one boy.

Everybody on the bus laughed—everybody but Jay. He cupped his hand harder against his pocket.

"Chee! Chee! Chee!" fiddled Cricket.

"Maybe Towhead down there in front has that cricket," said another boy in the back of the bus.

Everybody on the bus looked at Jay.

Jay crowded against the window. He pressed his hand hard against his pocket. He looked straight ahead.

"Chee! Chee! Chee!" fiddled Cricket.

"I'd like to see Teacher when that cricket starts singing in school," said someone else.

Everybody on the bus laughed very loud—everybody but Jay.

When the bus reached the schoolhouse it stopped.

Jay waited until all the other boys and girls had got off. Then, pressing his hand against his pocket, he too climbed off.

He stood wondering where to go.

The driver smiled at him. "You belong in that room just inside the front door," he said to Jay. "Good luck with your cricket!" he added.

Jay looked at the other boys and girls in the schoolyard. They were calling to one another. They were laughing and talking.

Jay kept close to the fence as he made his way around them.

He found his room.

He found Teacher inside the room.

He told her his name.

He sat at the desk she pointed out to him.

Jay kept his hand pressed over his pocket. He sat still and waited.

A bell rang.

Teacher began talking to the children. The children listened. The room was very quiet.

"Chee!" fiddled Cricket.

Jay pressed his hand against his pocket to quiet Cricket.

"Chee! Chee! Chee!" fiddled Cricket.

The children turned in their seats. They giggled.

Teacher stopped talking. She looked about the room.

"Does someone have a cricket in this room?" she asked.

No one answered.

Teacher began talking again.

"Chee! Chee!" fiddled Cricket.

Teacher left the front of the room. She walked
up and down between the rows of desks. As she
walked, she talked to the children. As she talked,
she listened.

She reached Jay's desk.

"Chee! Chee!" fiddled Cricket.

"Jay," Teacher asked, "do you have that
cricket?"

Jay swallowed hard. He nodded his head.

"You'd better put it outside," said Teacher.
"It's disturbing the class."

Jay sat very still. He looked at his desk. He pressed his hand hard against his pocket. He felt Cricket squirming.

"Jay," said Teacher, "put the cricket outside."

Still Jay sat. Still he looked at his desk.

"Jay," said Teacher, "aren't you going to put the cricket outside?"

Jay shook his head.

"Why not?" asked Teacher.

"I couldn't find him again," said Jay.

"Put him outside anyway," said Teacher. She waited.

Jay swallowed hard. He glanced up at Teacher. Then he looked at his desk again.

"You could find another cricket, couldn't you?" asked Teacher.

Jay shook his head. "It wouldn't be this one," he said.

"Chee! Chee!" fiddled Cricket.

Jay looked up at Teacher.

"Jay," said Teacher, "is this cricket your friend?"

Jay nodded his head.

"I see," said Teacher.

Teacher walked slowly to the front of the room.

"Boys and girls," she said, "this morning Jay has brought a cricket to class. It is something special. It is his friend. Jay, will you come to the front of the room and show the boys and girls your cricket? You can put him under this glass," she said.

She turned a water glass upside down on her desk.

Jay walked to the front of the room.

He took Cricket from his pocket.

He put Cricket under the upside-down glass.

"Tell the class about your cricket, Jay," said Teacher. "How did you catch him?"

Jay told the class how he had caught Cricket in the cow pasture.

The boys and girls asked Jay many questions.

"How long have you had Cricket?"

"What does he eat?"

"Where does he sleep?"

"How high can he jump?"

"Can he do tricks?"

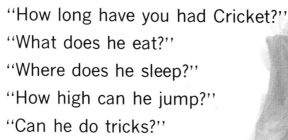

Jay answered all their questions.

"What makes him sing?" asked one girl.

"He doesn't sing," said Jay. "He fiddles with his wings."

"Tell him to fiddle now," said all the boys and girls.

"He likes to fiddle in the dark," explained Jay. "That's why he was fiddling in my pocket. It's dark in there."

"Does Cricket fiddle especially for you sometimes?" asked Teacher.

"Every night," said Jay.

"You may put Cricket back in your pocket now, Jay," said Teacher. "If he fiddles, he won't disturb us."

"What are you going to bring next, Jay?" asked a boy.

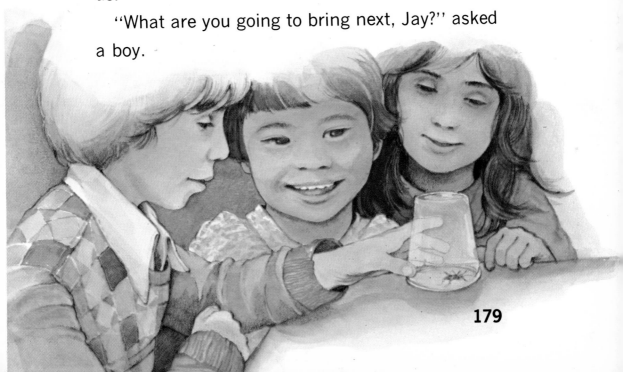

Jay thought of the stone with the print of a fern on one side. He thought of the gray goose feather. He thought of the Indian arrowhead.

He thought of the hickory nut, and of the smell of it that tingled in his nose like the smell of the first frost.

He thought of the beans.

He thought of the cicada fiddling high notes in the summer heat.

He thought of the russet apples and the red apples growing on the same tree—sweet and sour, sweet and sour.

He thought again of the beans—white, striped with red speckles, and, in his hand, cool, like morning.

"Beans," he said.

Rebecca Caudill

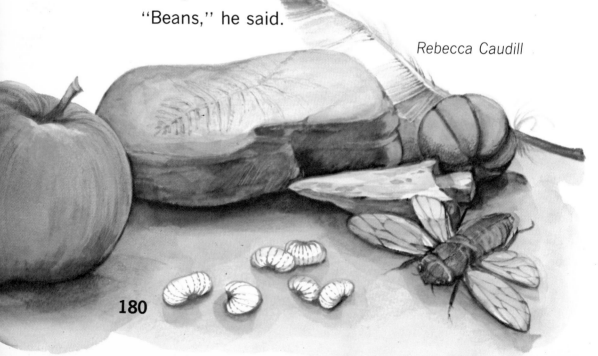

A Most Unusual Pet

Suppose you could have any pet you wanted—whether there really was such an animal or not. Would it be a giraffe with a red saddle like Maria's, a Snortsnoot, or a Blooplebee? What would it eat? Where would it sleep? Where would it play?

Think of a very unusual pet. When you have a pet in mind, describe it to your classmates. Your pet could be as unusual as a pink hippopotamus who eats only chocolate candy bars, likes to sleep in the bathtub, and runs through the flowers in the park.

On another sheet fill in the blanks for the pet you are thinking of.

I would like to have a _____ who would eat only _____. It would like to _____ and then _____. I would name my pet _____ and would keep it in _____.

Now that you have told about your unusual pet, try to make up a story about something that happened to the two of you one day.

Speaking of Dinosaurs

Discovering Dinosaurs

When you tell somebody that something happened a long time ago you may mean that it happened a few years ago or before you were born or even before your parents were born. But when you read that dinosaurs lived a long time ago it means that they lived a long, long, LONG time ago. That means long before your parents were born and even long before your grandparents were born or your great great grandparents. Long before there were any towns. Before there were books. Before there were people. Before there was anything that you can see from your window now—except clouds and sky. And that *is* a very long time.

Dinosaurs lived on the earth millions and millions of years before there were any people. Nobody ever went dinosaur hunting because there wasn't any person living on the earth to go. So of course nobody ever met a live dinosaur in the woods or anywhere else.

Dinosaurs lived on the earth for a LONG, LONG, LONG time. They lived on many parts of the earth. Many of them lived on the part of the earth that is now the United States—in Wyoming, Colorado, Utah, Arizona, Texas, Montana, and in many, many other states. Of course, there was no United States then.

Dinosaurs ruled the animal world when they lived, millions of years ago. Some of them were the biggest of all animals. They were the fiercest animals. And there were more dinosaurs than any other kind of four-footed animals.

In those days there were no horses, no cows, no sheep, no squirrels. There were no birds. There were frogs and toads, but they were not like the ones we have today. There were fish in the sea, but they were not like our bass and trout. There were big sea turtles. Even though there were other animals on land and in the sea, those days of long ago were the days of the dinosaurs.

187

Even the trees and other plants did not look then as they do now. There were trees and bushes that looked like palms and evergreens, but there were no oaks and maples. There were no garden flowers and no vegetables. The animals and plants were very different then from the animals and plants that you see when you walk in the woods and fields. Dinosaurs lived in a very different world from ours.

What did a dinosaur look like? That's like asking, "What does a bird look like?" It depends upon what kind of a bird you are asking about. There are many kinds of birds. There are owls and bluebirds and ostriches. But bluebirds don't look like owls and owls don't look like ostriches. But bluebirds, owls and ostriches are all birds. There were many kinds of dinosaurs too. And they didn't look alike any more than birds do. There were thousands of kinds of dinosaurs.

Dinosaurs were all sizes and shapes. Some were terrible giant animals that were big enough to look over a house and see what was in the back yard. But of course there were no houses and no back yards in the days of the dinosaurs. Some of them were the biggest land animals that have ever lived on the earth. Some were as small as a cat that can scramble under your back yard fence. And some were middle-sized, like sheep or pigs. Some were a little larger, about the size of horses and cows. Some were still a little larger, about the size of elephants. Many of them were bigger than you can believe.

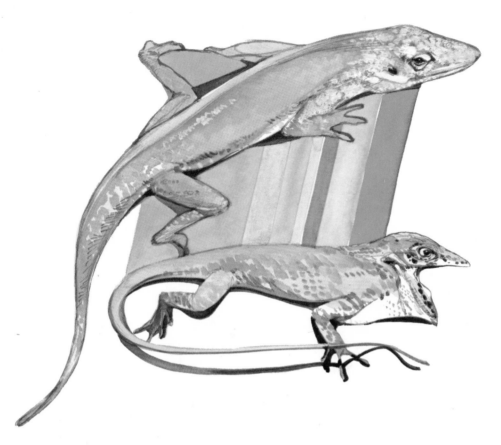

All dinosaurs were reptiles.[1] There are reptiles living on the earth today, but they do not look at all like the dinosaurs did. Snakes and lizards and turtles are all reptiles. Crocodiles and alligators are reptiles too. They all have scales or hard parts on the outside of their bodies, and they breathe with lungs.

1 reptiles (REP-tilz)

Dinosaurs spent much of their time roaming over the land looking for something to eat. Some ate smaller animals. Some of the large dinosaurs ate smaller dinosaurs, and some of the large ones killed and ate each other. Some ate plants of all kinds, and others were both plant eaters and animal eaters, and still others were only meat eaters.

The big ones lumbered along as they looked for animals and plants to eat. The little ones could run fast, and probably did. They chased other animals or went from one place to another to find new plants to eat.

Some dinosaurs spent much of their time in swamps or in the water. They found food there because the animals and plants they liked to eat lived there. Some kinds of dinosaurs got away from their enemies by hurrying into the water when enemies were after them.

Many of the dinosaurs walked on two strong hind legs. Their hind legs were longer than their front legs. Their hind legs were good for walking and their front legs for grabbing and holding food. There were long strong claws on their hind legs and on their front legs too. These claws were used to catch and hold and tear their food.

Many of the dinosaurs had strong teeth. Some had teeth for meat eating but more of them had plant-eating teeth. Can you tell what an animal eats by looking at its teeth? Look at your dog's teeth and you will see sharp teeth for biting and tearing meat. Some of the teeth help the dog to hold on to food. Some of them help to grind meat and get it ready for the dog to swallow.

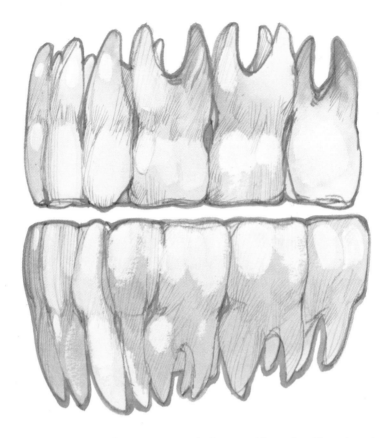

Your own teeth are good for eating both plants and meat. The front ones are for biting. The back ones are for chewing. Feel them with your tongue and you can tell how they are different from each other.

There were many exciting kinds of dinosaurs. The next story tells you about a few of the largest ones.

Glenn O. Blough

Dinosaur Differences

One of the first dinosaurs was very big. Its body was as big as a truck or a small airplane. It had a long neck, a long tail, and a very long name. Its name was Brontosaurus.[1]

Brontosaurus liked the water. The dinosaur stayed in the water as much as it could because it was easy for it to walk in water. But it was hard for Brontosaurus to walk on land because its body was so heavy.

[1] Brontosaurus (brahn-tə-SAWR-uhss); also called Apatosaurus (ə-pa-toh-SAWR-uhss)

Brontosaurus found much of its food in the water. The dinosaur needed a lot of food because it was so big. Brontosaurus was safe in water. But it was not safe on land because there was another dinosaur on land that wanted to eat it. This dinosaur was called Allosaurus.[1]

When Allosaurus came near, Brontosaurus ran away. It ran through the mud and splashed through the water. Allosaurus could not swim so it could not follow Brontosaurus into the deep water. When Brontosaurus got to the deep water, it was safe.

[1] Allosaurus (al-ə-SAWR-uhss); also called Antrodemus (an-trə-DEEM-uhss)

199

But some of the first dinosaurs did not live near water. One of these was Stegosaurus.[1] It lived on dry land and ate the plants there. Stegosaurus was one of the first dinosaurs to have armor. It had armor on its back. The armor went all the way from the head to the tail and helped to keep Stegosaurus safe. Stegosaurus had a tail that kept it safe, too. On the end of the tail there were four long spikes. No other dinosaur wanted to get near those spikes. Not even Allosaurus. So if it was not very, VERY hungry, Allosaurus left Stegosaurus alone.

1 Stegosaurus (steg-ə-SAWR-uhss)

Not all the dinosaurs lived at the same time. Scientists say that Brontosaurus, Allosaurus, Stegosaurus and many other dinosaurs lived for millions and millions of years. Then, one by one, they died out. Brontosaurus died out. Allosaurus died out. Stegosaurus died out, too.

But many new dinosaurs came to take their place. One of these new dinosaurs lived in the water, or near the water. The name of this dinosaur was Trachodon.[1] Trachodon was a big dinosaur. It was as tall as a tall tree. It ate only plants and leaves. Trachodon had a long, wide tail that helped it to swim very well.

[1] Trachodon (TRAK-ə-don)

Some of the new dinosaurs had horns. One kind of dinosaur had three horns. It had a little horn on the end of its nose and two big horns above its eyes. Its name was Triceratops.[1] Triceratops was a big animal, much bigger than a horse or a cow. It had small teeth and ate only plants and leaves. But because of its horns, Triceratops was not afraid of any other animal. It was not even afraid of the most terrible dinosaur of all—Tyrannosaurus.[2]

[1] Triceratops (trigh-SEHR-ə-tops)
[2] Tyrannosaurus (ti-ran-ə-SAWR-uhss)

Tyrannosaurus was one of the last of the dinosaurs. It ate only other animals. It stood 20 feet tall. Tyrannosaurus could look over the top of a tall tree. From its nose to its tail it was almost 50 feet long. This dinosaur was as long as a big truck. Its teeth were as long as a person's hand. And its mouth was full of teeth. Tyrannosaurus was probably the most terrible animal that ever lived on the land.

When Tyrannosaurus came, the other dinosaurs ran. Some ran into the water. Some ran under plants or behind trees. All the dinosaurs ran—all but one. Triceratops did not run. Triceratops stood right where it was. It saw Tyrannosaurus. It saw the terrible teeth. But Triceratops was not afraid. If Tyrannosaurus was looking for a fight, Triceratops would give it one. Most times, Tyrannosaurus went away and left Triceratops alone. There were other dinosaurs to catch and eat. Other dinosaurs that were not as big as Triceratops. Other dinosaurs that did not have two big horns.

But if Tyrannosaurus was very, VERY hungry, it stayed to fight. And what a terrible fight that must have been. The most terrible fight two animals ever had. Many times Tyrannosaurus won. Many times it was too strong for Triceratops, but not always. There were many times when Triceratops won, too. Triceratops must have been a brave animal. Any animal that stayed to fight with Tyrannosaurus must have been brave.

Then after millions and millions of years, something happened to the dinosaurs. All at once, they began to die out again. But this time no new dinosaurs came to take their place. Trachodon died out. Brave Triceratops died out. Even Tyrannosaurus, the most terrible animal that ever lived, died out too. At last there was not one dinosaur left in the world.

No one knows why all the dinosaurs died out. All we can do is guess what may have happened.

William Wise

Whatever Happened to All Those Dinosaurs?

This is a question that is easy to answer. They all died. There's not one left on the earth. They have been dead for millions of years. But when you ask "*Why* did they all die?" you are asking a very hard question. It is such a hard question that the best scientists in the world are not sure of the answer. They have ideas that may explain why these large, fierce dinosaurs all died. But no one is sure.

The first thing to remember is that the climate on the earth has not always been the same. It has changed from warm to cold and wet to dry and in other ways too. Once part of the United States and all of Canada were covered with a layer of ice many feet thick. Once many parts of the United States were covered with water. The earth has changed many times since animals and plants first lived on it.

Many scientists think that these changes in the climate may have caused dinosaurs to die. When the climate changed, many of the plants could no longer live. When the plants were gone the dinosaurs' food was gone. Even the dinosaurs who ate animals could not live if many of the plants died. This was because many of the animals they ate for food lived on plants. Scientists believe that changes in climate may be one of the reasons that dinosaurs died.

But many scientists think there were other reasons why dinosaurs died. Perhaps something happened to their eggs. Maybe some other animals found their eggs and ate so many that there were no more young dinosaurs. Or perhaps the change in climate kept the eggs from hatching. Some scientists believe that some dinosaurs may have eaten the eggs of other dinosaurs. But why would this happen all of a sudden? This is a puzzle that scientists have not solved.

Animals must be able to survive in the place where they live. Most water animals must be able to move about in the water. Water animals usually have fins or flippers or something else to push themselves through the water. They need gills to breathe under the water. Water animals cannot live on land.

If animals live on land they need legs or
something else to move with. They need lungs
for breathing. They must be able to protect
themselves against their enemies. Land animals
cannot live in water.

If the place where animals live changes, then the animals must change too. This takes a long, long time. Animals that live in water cannot suddenly live on land. Perhaps the dinosaurs were not able to change fast enough to keep up with the changes that took place on the earth. Perhaps that is why they all died. So when the swamps and seas and ponds dried up, the dinosaurs died.

Even though many dinosaurs were very large, many of them had very small heads and almost all of them had very small brains for such large animals. Some scientists think that this may have been one reason that they all died. Their brains were not very good, so perhaps they could not get away from their enemies or protect themselves in other ways. Maybe they just didn't have the brains to stay alive.

Glenn O. Blough

215

How Do We Know About Dinosaurs?

Finding Clues

If the dinosaurs died millions of years ago, and no one was alive to see them, then how do we know so much about them? How do we know what they looked like?

We know about dinosaurs from their bones. We have found many dinosaur bones. We have even found their eggs and their footprints. Does this seem hard to believe? Perhaps. The scientists themselves were surprised when the first bones were discovered.

But over the years the scientists learned much about the story of the dinosaurs. They worked very slowly. Sometimes they spent years putting together the bones from just one dinosaur.

The story began in 1818. The United States was a very young country then. Not a single railroad had been built. People traveled by wagon, by boat, on horses, or on their own feet.

In 1818 some strange bones were dug up in the valley of the Connecticut River. No one knew what kind of animal they had come from.

A few years later, a woman was exploring some rocks in Sussex, England. She came across some strange teeth, which she thought were interesting. She showed them to her husband, the scientist Dr. Gideon Mantell.

Dr. Mantell had never seen anything like these big teeth. He shared his wife's discovery with other scientists. They said the teeth had probably come from a rhinoceros.[1] But who ever heard of a rhinoceros in England? The rhinoceros belonged in Africa and Asia.

The Mantells took some tools to the place where the teeth had been found. They dug very carefully and found a number of strange bones.

1 rhinoceros (righ-NOSS-ər-əss)

They studied the bones for a long time. Finally Dr. Mantell decided the bones had come from a large reptile. The teeth looked like those of a living lizard, the iguana.[1]

Later another scientist gave this strange reptile a general name: dinosaur. Dinosaur means "terrible lizard."

Even before the first dinosaur bones were dug up, strange footprints had been discovered in solid rock. Nobody ever thought that animals had made them.

The first footprints were reported in 1802. A Connecticut farmer was plowing his corn field. His plow struck a buried stone. He dug it out. It was marked with tracks like those of a large bird.

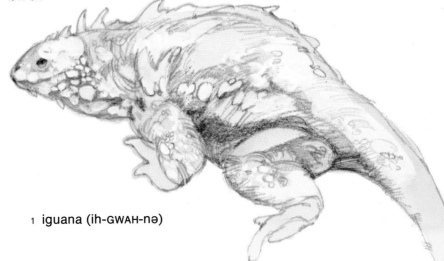

[1] iguana (ih-GWAH-nə)

Other stones with tracks were found. Years later people learned that the tracks had not been left by birds. They had been made by dinosaurs that walked on their hind legs. These dinosaurs had three toes on each foot.

But how could the dinosaurs make tracks in hard stone? They couldn't. The tracks were made along the edge of a river or a shallow bay of the sea. Sometimes the water would spread over the shore, turning the hard ground into mud. Then the water would fall back.

The dinosaurs walked through the mud. Then the sun dried it and baked it. The footprints were as plain as a dog's tracks in a fresh concrete sidewalk.

When the water rose again, the footprints were filled with fine sand. After a great many years, the mud turned into hard rock. The giant tracks were still there. The water brought in more sand and mud, burying the tracks.

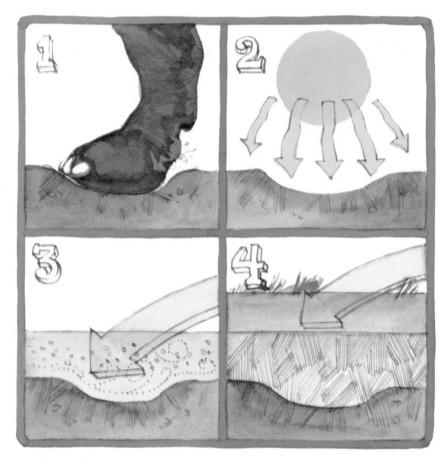

It was millions of years later that the Connecticut farmer plowed up the famous stone. There were the same tracks. They had been made by one of the thousands of dinosaurs that used to feed on plants in the river valley.

Dinosaur footprints have been found in many places besides Connecticut. Some of them are as long as the arm of a boy or girl.

Bones Become Fossils

Scientists have learned much about dinosaurs by studying their bones. These bones have been buried for millions of years and have turned to stone. They are called fossils.

In Arizona, a whole forest was turned to stone. It is called the Petrified Forest. There you can see hundreds of fossil trees lying on the ground. Some are whole. Others have broken into large chunks or small pieces. All of this wood was once buried. It became stone after thousands of years.

Some fossils show the print of leaves, ferns, and even insects. Long ago they lay in mud. After thousands of years the mud turned to stone.

These fossils tell us what the world was like millions of years ago. Fossils of palm trees and giant ferns have been found with the bones of dinosaurs. So we know they all lived at the same time.

Palm trees need warm weather. Giant ferns need plenty of rain. So there must have been more heat and rain than we have now.

At first, fossils were found only by mistake. They might be found on hillsides where roads were being built. Or when a basement was being dug. Or when a farmer plowed a field.

Usually fossils are not found on top of the ground. When scientists began to look for fossils, they hunted in deep valleys and canyons. They looked for places where the rocks had been washed bare by rain and running water.

The best place to look for fossils is desert country. The ground is not protected by trees and grass. Underneath there may be bones that have been buried for millions of years.

The desert gets much wind and some rain. In some places, the soil is blown away by the wind and carried away by the water. Then the bones underneath can be seen. This is where the work of the scientist who studies bones really begins.

Roy Chapman Andrews

Solving the Puzzle

Paleontologists[1] are scientists who know many things about rocks and how they were made. They are especially interested in the rocks that are made when mud and clay and sand settle out of water. These rocks are the ones most likely to have fossils in them.

1 paleontologists (pay-lee-on-TOL-ə-jəsts)

Paleontologists know a lot about where different kinds of rocks are found. When paleontologists go out on a scientific detective trip, they go where the right kinds of rocks are. Then they begin to look. They may find first a few small bones or teeth or other small fossils. They may find only tiny chips from bones, or they may find a part of a bone sticking out of the rock. Then they really begin to do some detective work. They may dig some of the rock away and find that the bone is not so small after all. It may turn out to be a very large bone. It may turn out to be many bones. It may be a whole group of bones that can be fit together and made into an animal frame. This bone frame is called a skeleton.[1]

1 skeleton (SKEL-ə-tən)

Digging these bones out of the ground or rock is not an easy job. Paleontologists can't do it as you would dig up a rock that you wanted to move out of your back yard. You would use a pick and shovel and other large tools. Paleontologists cannot do this because they may break the bones in the rocks. They often start by digging around the rock until they can see the outside of the bones. Then they dig under it very carefully and finally lift it out.

Paleontologists can't just dump the fossil rock into the back seat of their cars either. They must be sure that they won't break any of the bones, which may be as easy to break as an egg. When the bones are broken, they may be useless for study.

The fossil rock is usually covered with pieces of cloth and a paste that gets hard the way plaster for a wall gets hard. The paleontologist presses the cloth and paste into the rough places in the rock and covers it with cloth and plaster so that none of the bones will stick out and get broken. This cloth and hard paste protect the bones on their trip back to the laboratory. Often many large pieces of fossil rock are brought back from one scientific detective trip.

In the laboratory paleontologists begin to chip the rock away from the bones to see what they have really found. The work goes slowly and must be done very carefully with special tools. Finally the bones are separated from the rock and cleaned up.

Sometimes the bones fit together into a skeleton just as they come from the rock. But often they don't. Then the paleontologist must use everything known about animals and bones and fossils to help make a skeleton.

Paleontologists must know a lot about how bones fit together to make an animal skeleton. They study skeletons of all kinds of animals. They use whatever they know about bones and skeletons to fit together the bones that have been found. They fit the bones together the way you fit the parts of a puzzle together. Sometimes they find that the bones will not make a skeleton at all. But sometimes they discover that some of these bones will fit other bones found in another place and at another time. They may not be from the same animal but they may be from the same kind of animal.

Animal skeletons have been made from bones that have come from many different places. Scientists once worked more than fifty years to find the bones to make one skeleton in a museum. They collected the bones from dozens of different places.

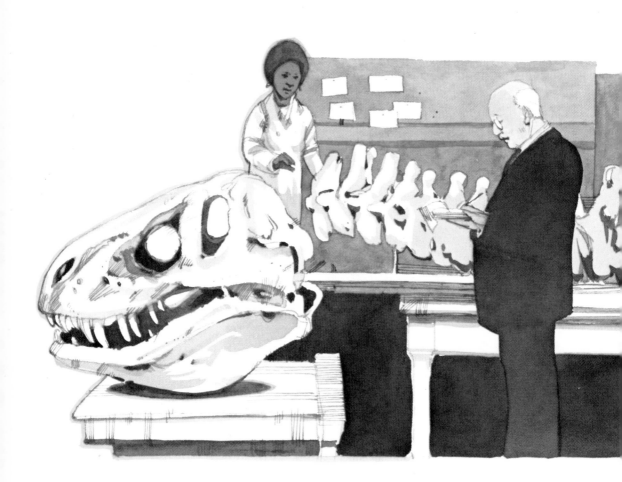

If you saved all the bones of a chicken and tried to put them together to make a skeleton, you would see that it is a very hard job. It is hard to tell how the bones fit together. It is even hard when you know what the skeleton of a chicken looks like. But suppose you had a pile of bones of an animal you had never seen. Then the job would be much harder. Remember that no one has ever seen a live dinosaur, and so scientists must work very carefully and do plenty of thinking about these bone puzzles. They must work the way you do when you are trying to put together a picture puzzle and you can't find the picture.

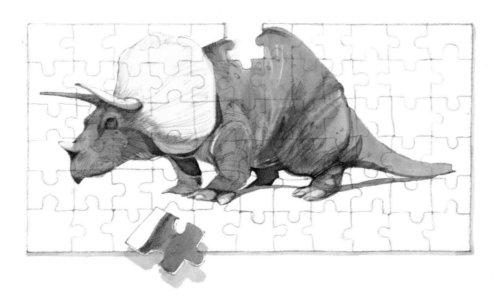

Paleontologists are like other scientists. They look carefully at things and they think about what they see. They sometimes must say, "I'm not sure about this. This may be the way these bones fit together. But it may not be." Years later someone may find the same kind of skeleton with all the bones in one place. Then the first scientist can be sure that the skeleton is put together correctly. But if the skeleton does not look like the new one, it must be changed.

Paleontologists do not rush through their work. They often say, "Wait a minute now. Let's be sure. Maybe this is true and maybe it is not. Let's get more facts." Scientists must work this way no matter what kind of puzzles they are trying to solve.

Glenn O. Blough

When Dinosaurs Were Roaming

A hundred million years ago
   In what is now Wyoming,
Midst Mesozoic jungle swamps
   The dinosaurs were roaming.

Some fed upon the leafy plants
   That grew along the shore,
While some ate those who ate the plants,
   Then looked around for more.

Some walked upon all fours, as you'd
   Expect of such a beast.
Some walked two-legged, like a man.
   There all resemblance ceased.

A few were small as dog or cat,
   But most were quite enormous.
Take BRONTOSAURUS, eighty feet
   In length, as books inform us.

239

So big was Brontosaurus that
    One brain would not suffice.
Besides the wee one in his head
    He had, and this was nice,

Another brain, or bunch of nerves,
    Placed rather near the rear
That doubtless had the duties of
    Assistant engineer.

And when an enemy drew near,
    This Brontosaurus slid
Into the water hurriedly,
    And there he wisely hid.

Who was this enemy he feared?
    Why was it that he fled him?
Well, it was ALLOSAURUS, and
    He had a right to dread him.

For Allosaurus, huge and high,
   On two hind feet went zipping.
His toes were tipped with hooklike nails
   That badly needed clipping.

His bite was very special too.
   His jaws were chomping whizzers.
His lower teeth and uppers worked
   Much like the blades of scissors.

He munched and crunched and crunched and munched
   With monstrous appetite,
And those who fled him did not wish
   A bit to be a bite.

"Look out, look out for Allosaur—!"
   Each creature warned his friend.
Should any stumble as they ran,
   Too bad—that was the end.

241

TRICERATOPS was well equipped
    With horns. His numbered three,
One on his nose's tip and two
    Where eyebrows ought to be.

And as for shields, to shield his neck
    From those who tried to grab it
He had a fancy bony frill
    He wore from force of habit.

What took the pleasure out of life
    For every living thing?
TYRANNOSAURUS REX. (The ''rex''
    Means he was boss, or king.)

A tyrant was Tyrannosaurus,
    Forever seeking food.
The others, though they loved to chew,
    Weren't fond of being chewed.

242

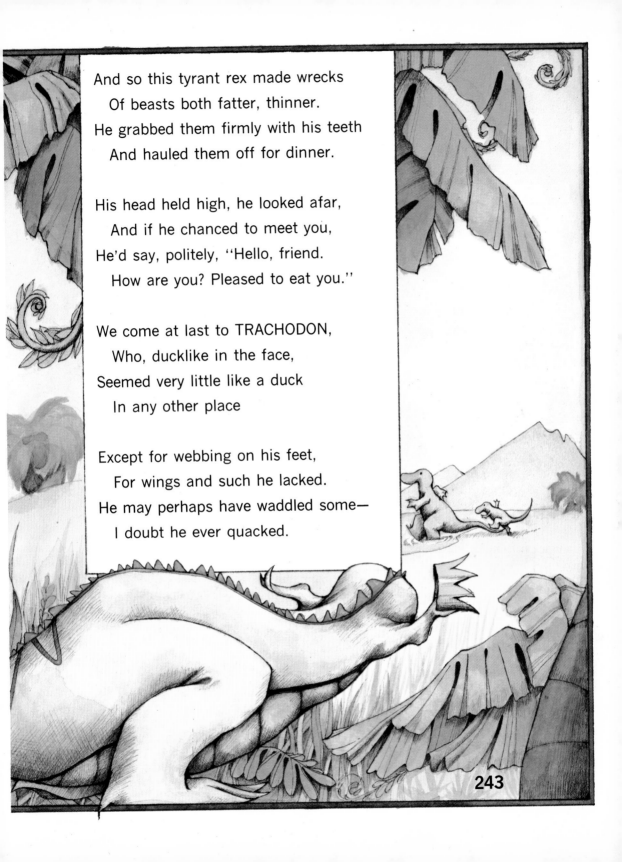

And so this tyrant rex made wrecks
   Of beasts both fatter, thinner.
He grabbed them firmly with his teeth
   And hauled them off for dinner.

His head held high, he looked afar,
   And if he chanced to meet you,
He'd say, politely, "Hello, friend.
   How are you? Pleased to eat you."

We come at last to TRACHODON,
   Who, ducklike in the face,
Seemed very little like a duck
   In any other place

Except for webbing on his feet,
   For wings and such he lacked.
He may perhaps have waddled some—
   I doubt he ever quacked.

243

This Trachodon stayed in or near
   The water all the time.
With ever-eager outstretched bill
   He slip-slopped through the slime.

He searched, you see, for tender slugs
   And cuttlefish and crabs,
All which he ate, along with plants,
   In gulps and dibs and dabs.

What made the dinosaurs die out
   Despite their strength and size?
Some blame it on their little brains
   And lack of enterprise.

Give thought, then, to the dinosaurs,
   Whom one no longer dreads.
They used their teeth and used their claws
   But didn't use their heads.

Richard Armour

Your-Own-O-Saurus

The names of dinosaurs are not just funny-sounding, strange words with no meaning. The different word-parts that make up the names of dinosaurs do have meaning. For example, *saurus* means *lizard*. *Dino* means *terrible*. So *dino·saurus* means *terrible lizard*. *Bronto·saurus* means *thunder lizard*.

Now that you know how the names of dinosaurs are made, read the sentences. Then, on another sheet, fill in what you think each dinosaur should be called.

This dinosaur has fifty legs and can run as fast as a horse. It is a ———————.

This dinosaur spends twelve hours a day eating. It will eat anything it can reach or catch. It is a ———————.

This dinosaur is very lazy and likes to spend most of the time sleeping. It is a ———————.

How would you describe a sneako·saurus? A grino·saurus? A singo·saurus?

246

Starlight and Sagebrush

247

SLUE-FOOT SUE
THE RAINMAKER

Pecos Bill was a very famous cowboy. So famous that other cowboys used to talk about him. "Pecos Bill," they said, "can throw a loop further than any cowboy. He can lasso a dozen cows safely in a single bundle. Pecos Bill is the greatest cowboy in the West."

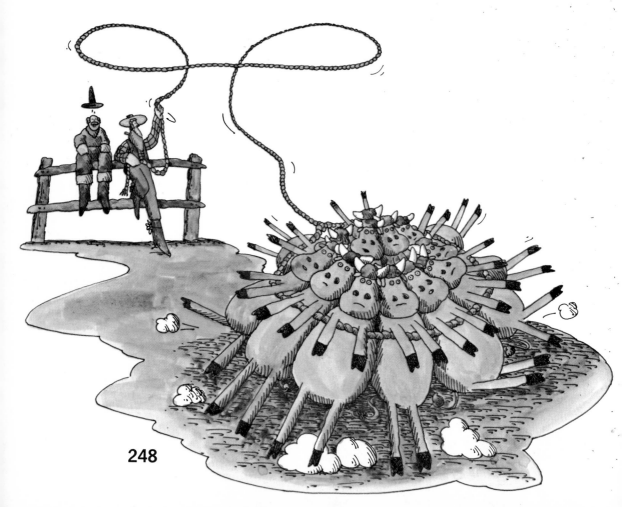

Pecos Bill broke many wild horses to the saddle. His favorite was a mustang called Widow-Maker. Other cowboys had tried to tame Widow-Maker but they failed. The horse had bucked and twisted so much that they were thrown off his back. Sometimes they were hurt badly. Only Pecos Bill could ride Widow-Maker.

Late one clear night, Bill rode Widow-Maker along the Pecos River. Thousands of stars were mirrored in the stream. Bill felt lonely. Then a round moon rose. It made the night as clear as day.

Bill saw a sight he would never forget. Down the shining river came a pretty girl riding bareback on a Texas catfish. The catfish was rearing and plunging and bucking. But the girl was riding him smoothly and easily. When she saw Bill, she edged the fish close to the river bank.

"My name is Slue-Foot Sue," she said. "I am the champion girl rider in all the west."

"You are very pretty too," said Bill.

"I like being a good rider better than being pretty," said Sue.

That afternoon Bill and Sue sat and talked. By the end of the day they had decided to get married.

Folks came from miles around to the big wedding party the next week. For wedding gifts all the guests gave Bill and Sue lassos.

Slue-Foot Sue and Pecos Bill lived happily for a few months at their ranch beside the Pecos River. But no rains came in the spring. The yellow waters of the Pecos began to dry up. Not a drop of water fell from the sky. Sue had to keep her catfish in the old swimming hole. The rest of the river was too shallow for him to swim in. Widow-Maker galloped up the mountain every day. He drank the cold water from the melting snow near the top.

One night, all the Texas stars looked as if they had been cleaned and polished.

"Bill," Sue said to her husband. "Do we still have all those lassos we got for wedding presents?"

"They're in the woodshed," said Pecos Bill.

"Please get them," said Slue-Foot Sue. "I want you to tie them all together and make the longest lasso in the world. We are going to climb the mountain and I want you to bring the lasso along."

Bill looked puzzled.

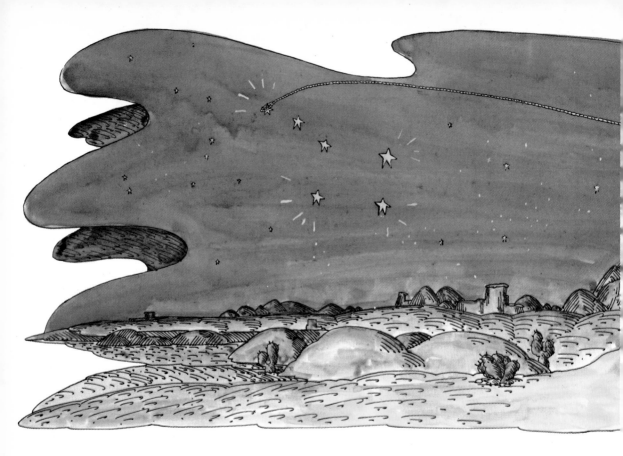

At the top of the mountain the stars looked even nearer and brighter than before.

Sue asked, "Do you see the Little Dipper?"

"Yes," said Bill.

"Can you throw our lasso over the handle?" asked Sue. "Then if we both pull hard enough we might tip the dipper. The water inside would pour out."

"A good idea!" shouted Bill. "I can rope it. Just give me room to get the loop started!"

Soon the lasso was circling Bill's head. It made a singing sound through the bright air. Bill kept adding more rope to its length. At last, with one great toss, Bill let it go. Up, up it went toward the stars of the Little Dipper. Sue and Bill waited. It seemed a long time before the line suddenly tightened.

"I've got it," shouted Bill. "Now pull."

Pull they did, as hard as they could. Slowly the handle of the Little Dipper began to turn. Bill and Sue pulled even harder and the handle moved a little more. All night they tugged and tugged at the long rope.

Finally Sue said, "The Little Dipper's tipped enough. The water must be spilling. Let's tie the lasso fast and go home."

Daylight had begun to appear. Then suddenly there came a spatter of raindrops as big as oranges. Soon a steady stream of rain poured from the Dipper.

Bill and Sue walked home wet and happy. The falling rain washed the dusty brown trees and turned them green. The shining Pecos River overflowed its banks. Widow-Maker was drinking from it. Sue's catfish swam about joyfully.

Suddenly the rays of the rising sun struck the falling water. The biggest rainbow ever seen anywhere arched across the Texas sky.

Elizabeth and Carl Carmer

A Peanut

A peanut sat on the railroad track,
His heart was all a-flutter—
Choo-choo train comes 'round the bend,
Toot toot! Peanut butter!

I Scream, You Scream

I scream,
You scream,
We all scream
for ICE CREAM.

I Eat My Peas With Honey

I eat my peas with honey,
I've done so all my life,
It makes the peas taste funny,
But it keeps them on my knife!

Fuzzy Wuzzy

Fuzzy Wuzzy was a bear,
Fuzzy Wuzzy had no hair,
Then Fuzzy Wuzzy wasn't fuzzy,
Was he?

Old Grumble

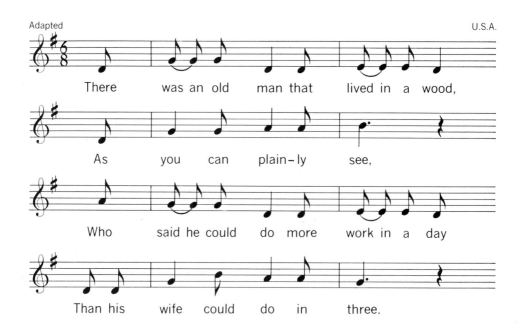

There was an old man that lived in a wood,

As you can plain-ly see,

Who said he could do more work in a day

Than his wife could do in three.

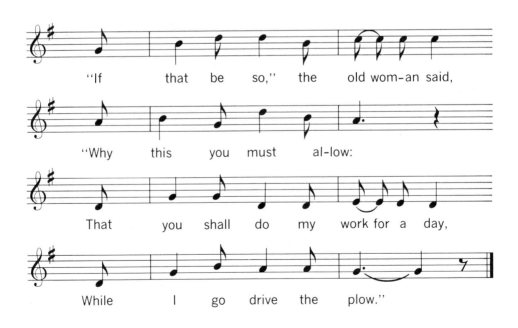

"If that be so," the old wom-an said,

"Why this you must al-low:

That you shall do my work for a day,

While I go drive the plow."

2. "But you must milk the tiny cow,
   For fear she should go dry;
   And you must feed the little pigs
   That are within the sty,
   And you must watch the bracket hen
   Lest she should lay astray;
   And you must wind the reel of yarn
   That I spun yesterday."

3. The old woman took the staff in her hand,
   And went to drive the plow,
   The old man took the pail in his hand,
   And went to milk the cow.
   But Tiny hinched, and Tiny flinched
   And Tiny cocked her nose,
   And Tiny hit the old man such a kick
   That the blood ran down to his toes.

4. 'Twas "Hey, my good cow,"
    and "Ho, my good cow,"
  And "Now, my good cow, stand still.
  If ever I milk this cow again,
  'Twill be against my will,"
  And when he had milked the tiny cow,
  For fear she would go dry,
  Why then he fed the little pigs,
  That were within the sty.

264

5. And then he watched the bracket hen
   Lest she should lay astray;
   But he forgot the reel of yarn
   His wife spun yesterday;
   He swore by all the leaves on the tree
   And all the stars in heaven,
   That his wife could do more work in a day
   Than he could do in seven.

Traditional

265

SAGEBRUSH TALES

Never-Stop,
the Post Hole Ghost

This whole story is true. Newspapers as far away as the *Rocky Mountain News* printed part of it. In my old stack of *The Frontier Press* you can read the full, true story.

Along in the 1880s boundary lines and fences got to be quite a problem in Texas. Ranchers had one set of rules. Sheepherders wanted things done another way. Well, tempers sometimes got heated, and strong words got said. It was clear that if you wanted a fence, you put it up first. You didn't talk it over with folks at the crossroad store. You just got your supplies and a good working crew and went at it. The faster, the better.

267

Nancy Owen lived over by Twin Springs. She'd set her mind on fencing the north-south line of her ranch. But she had quite a time. It wasn't that Miss Nancy lacked staying power. Some folks said she was as stubborn as her grandmother. That was saying quite a lot! But the ground was hard and rocky. The fencing crew made progress. But no one seemed to be able to dig post holes fast enough to keep ahead of the fencing crew.

One morning Miss Nancy was telling the crew to get a little more done that day. Just as the crew was about to set out, a stranger walked into camp. He was tall, but thin and stringy. From the looks of his coat and the way his dark beard was trimmed, they knew he was a stranger in these parts. He didn't come from anywhere near Twin Springs or any other place in Texas. And he didn't understand English or Spanish.

269

Miss Nancy, never happy with an idle hand around, decided to try him at digging post holes. Since she couldn't tell him what to do, she showed him. She stepped off 13 paces from the last post hole. She pointed with the shovel and the seven-foot iron bar used to pry out rocks. Then she pointed straight to the south.

Well, that stranger wasn't from Texas, but he could dig post holes. He set off like a streak. By noon he was 22 post holes ahead of the fencing crew. By noon of the second day, Miss Nancy had to ride way out to check on him. He was that far ahead of the crew. And that line of post holes was reaching straight south. At the end of the third day, they couldn't even find him. All they could see were those post holes of his in a beautiful straight line. They were all exactly 13 paces apart—all marching straight to the south.

They never did catch up to him. The fencing crew followed those post holes right to the end of Miss Nancy's ranch. The crew stopped there, but the post holes didn't. Miss Nancy followed more than a day's ride farther. She never saw the end. On and on as far as the eye could see, the line of post holes went straight south.

To this day no one is sure what happened to the stranger. On nights when the moon is full, more than one lonesome traveler has seen an old man with a flowing gray beard walking to the south. The old man stops every 13 paces trying to dig another hole. His worn out shovel is no bigger than a wooden spoon. His iron bar is no longer than a knitting needle. But still he digs.

That's the story of Never-Stop, the post hole ghost.

It's all true.

Traditional

All or Nothing

Most of the stories in our folklore are about ghosts but there are also many tales about hidden treasures.

How can it be otherwise in a place like ours? Spanish ships went down along the coast of Padre Island with their gold. The pirates left buried booty in the sand. There were few banks and that forced people to hide their money in wells, walls, caves, and even under the trees. There were bandits who had to get rid of their loot in a hurry. There is no question about it, there are hundreds of treasures . . . waiting for the lucky ones.

The following story took place in 1875 in a little town called Santa Cruz.

Cesario Balderas had gone deep into the hills looking for a cow he had lost. Suddenly he saw in front of him the entrance to a large cave. He went in and was very surprised. On the walls were drawings of animals.

He forgot about the paintings when he noticed, right in the middle of the floor, a big wooden chest filled to the brink with gold nuggets. He almost lost his mind at the sight of such wealth. He danced around the chest, laughing like a mad man. He even kissed nuggets of gold.

At that moment, he heard someone laughing. He said to himself, "That must be the echo of my own voice." But someone shouted, "All or nothing!"

Cesario tried to take it all. There was no way he could. The chest weighed a ton. In his frenzy he filled up his pockets and loaded his hat to the brim with gold nuggets. Then he rushed towards the entrance. The walls closed up on him. There was only solid rock in front of him.

There he was alone in the completely dark cave. The voice kept on repeating louder and louder, "All or nothing!"

He gave up. "I know I can't take it all, so it will be nothing!" He dropped the gold from his hands and emptied his hat. He took out handfuls of nuggets from his pockets. But he made sure to leave a few in each pocket.

The voice boomed louder than ever, "nothing!" This time, he obeyed and got rid of even the smallest nugget of gold.

The cave opened up again and Cesario ran out as fast as he could.

He left his shirt tied to a stick on top of the closest hill. He intended to come back and take it ALL next time.

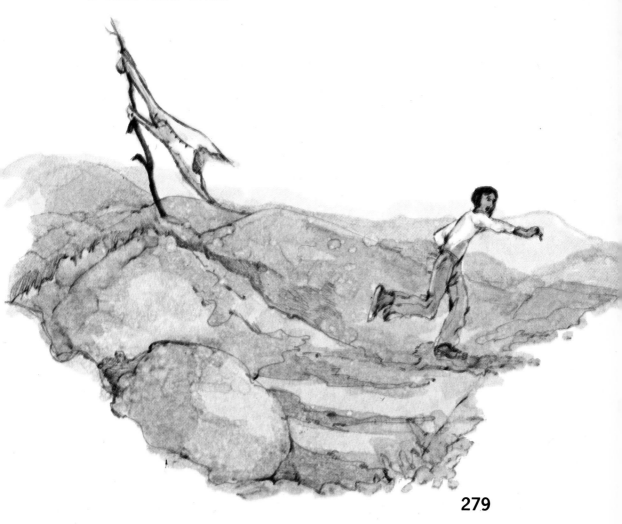

He returned a few hours later. He was ready. He had a wheelbarrow, a shovel, and a long rope. He searched for a long time and climbed dozens of hills. But he never found either the shirt or the entrance to the cave.

At sundown he finally came back to Santa Cruz. He stopped to tell his pals what he had seen in the hills.

They laughed at him and told him that funny things happen to people who stay too long in the sun. But Cesario was sure it had not been an illusion. "See these pockets? They were full of gold a few hours ago." As he said that, he turned his pockets inside out.

There was no more laughter. Cesario's pockets were still lined with gold dust!

That cave is still there in the hills with its treasure.

Juan Sauvageau

Ladles and Jelly Spoons

Ladles and jelly spoons:
I come before you
To stand behind you
And tell you something
I know nothing about.

Next Thursday,
The day after Friday,
There'll be a mothers meeting
For fathers only.

Wear your best clothes
If you haven't any,
And if you can come
Please stay home.

Admission is free,
You can pay at the door.
We'll give you a seat
So you can sit on the floor.

The Folk
Who Live in
BACKWARD TOWN

BACKWARD TOWN

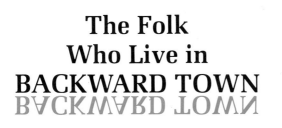

The folk who live in Backward Town
Are inside out and upside down.
They wear their hats inside their heads
And go to sleep beneath their beds.
They only eat the apple peeling
And take their walks across the ceiling.

Mary Ann Hoberman

283

Giant of the Timber

CHARACTERS

STORYTELLER

FIRST LOGGER

SECOND LOGGER

THIRD LOGGER

FOURTH LOGGER

FIFTH LOGGER

SIXTH LOGGER

PAUL'S MOTHER

PAUL'S FATHER

PAUL BUNYAN

A NEIGHBOR

BABE, the blue ox
   *(two people under
   a blanket)*

TIME

The nineteenth century.

PLACE

Different sections of the northern United States.

STORYTELLER

Paul Bunyan is one of our best known American folk heroes. Hundreds of stories have grown up around him. Some tell how he came down from Canada. Others say that he appeared first in the West. And still others, that he was born in New England and went west as a young man to clear land. Whether there really was a man of Paul's size doesn't matter. He was the spirit of the United States.

(*The* STORYTELLER *steps off and six children in jeans and wool shirts come in and sit down on the other side of the stage.*)

FIRST LOGGER

Sure, he was born in Minnesota. Didn't he clear land all across the state and start the biggest lumber business in the world?

SECOND LOGGER

Well, I heard how he came down from Canada. That's why he dug the St. Lawrence River. So many people got mixed up about which country was which that Paul thought a river would be a good way of telling them apart.

THIRD LOGGER

You're all wrong. He was born in Maine. My grandfather was there at the time and he told just why it was Paul left. It was like this . . . (*The* THIRD LOGGER *crosses the stage to the other side where he enters a scene with* PAUL'S MOTHER *and* FATHER.) Even when he was a little boy his father and mother knew he was no ordinary baby.

PAUL'S MOTHER

I think he's going to be president, Pa. He's grown faster and learned more in four months than any child I ever saw.

PAUL'S FATHER

He'll do big things, if he keeps on like this. Might be a sea captain or an explorer.

THIRD LOGGER

(*Now walking into the scene.*) How's the new baby, Mrs. Bunyan? I hear he's a big fellow.

PAUL'S MOTHER

(*Proudly.*) Land sakes, you haven't seen him yet! Eighty pounds when he was born, and growing like a weed.

PAUL'S FATHER

He's smart, too. All our children talked early but Paul, he's saying whole sentences already and he's only four months old.

THIRD LOGGER
Where is he? I'd like to see him.

PAUL'S MOTHER
Well, you'll have to come down to the beach. He got too big for me to handle, so his pa made a cradle for him out of a boat. We put him in it last week.

PAUL'S FATHER
It's in the bay where the waves can rock him all day long. Now all we have to do is carry his milk down to him.

THIRD LOGGER

But aren't you afraid he'll fall out?

PAUL'S FATHER

No, it's not very deep down there. And besides it's a flat-bottomed boat. You can see it from the door.

THIRD LOGGER

You mean that there's your baby? Why, he looks like a full grown man! Long black hair—and waving his arms around like that—

NEIGHBOR

(*Running in.*) Mr. Bunyan, Mr. Bunyan, come out quick! The baby, he—

PAUL'S FATHER

What's the matter?

289

PAUL'S MOTHER

What's happened? Did something happen to Paul? *(She starts off but stops when the* NEIGHBOR *speaks.)*

NEIGHBOR

No, *he's* all right. But he just rolled over in his cradle, the way babies do, and it's causing a tidal wave! You've got to move him before the whole village is flooded out!

(All exit and the THIRD LOGGER *returns to his circle.)*

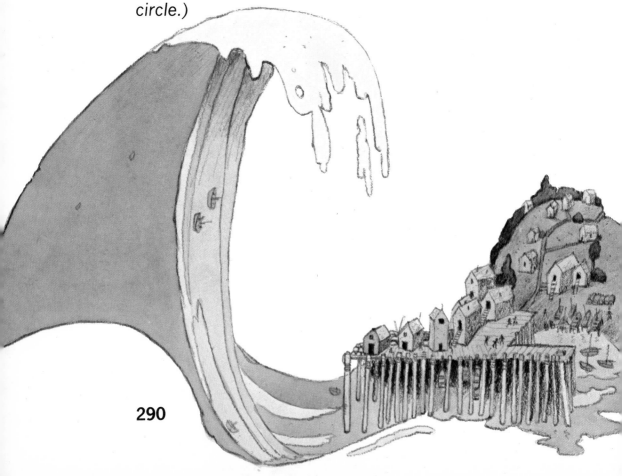

THIRD LOGGER

And that's the truth because my grandfather lived there and heard it. Well, after a few more scares like that, the state of Maine suggested politely that Paul go some place else.

FOURTH LOGGER

I can tell you where he went after that.

FIFTH LOGGER

He was smart enough but I heard they always had trouble with him in school because he was too big for the desks.

SIXTH LOGGER

Nothing was built for a child that size. So after a couple of years he quit school and just went on teaching himself.

FOURTH LOGGER

Well, next he was heard of was up in Canada. And that's why some folks say he came from those parts. It was the Winter of the Blue Snow and Paul was living by himself, trying to decide what to do with his life. He knew there was great work for him to do but up to then he wasn't sure just what it was.

(PAUL *walks out on the other side of the stage. He is the largest boy on stage.*)

292

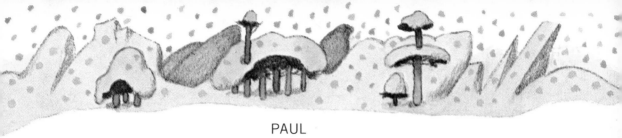

PAUL

Blue snow! They wouldn't believe it back in Maine if I told 'em. And if I sent them some, by the time it got there, it would be melted. *(Stops, then speaks again.)* Just as cold as it is blue, too. *(He walks a few steps.)* Thought I heard something. Sounded like an animal. Not very old and maybe hurt. Likely freezing in this weather. *(He calls in a big voice.)* Where are you? Can you hear me? *(Pause.)* Over here. *(He moves to the side of the stage and discovers a BLUE OX. It can be two people covered with a blue blanket and a paper bag mask on the head of the one in front.)* A little blue calf! Just a baby and out alone in all this weather. Seems to me you need food of some kind mighty quick. *(He pulls some bread out of his knapsack and offers it to the calf.)* That's right. If you eat like that, you'll grow up into a big blue ox. *(Thoughtfully.)* You know, you're alone and I'm alone. There's work in this world for both of us. Maybe, if we pull together, we'll discover what it is.

293

FOURTH LOGGER

And that's how Paul got Babe, the famous Blue Ox, that worked with him as long as he lived.

FIRST LOGGER

Everybody knows about the Blue Ox. Seemed like after that Paul knew that lumber was his business and Babe took to it like a duck to water. As fast as Paul chopped down the trees, Babe carried 'em off.

SIXTH LOGGER

And lots of other things happened too. Some of them good and some of them not so good.

FIRST LOGGER

But the thing about Paul was that he could turn a calamity into good luck. Like the time he made popcorn balls.

294

THIRD LOGGER

(Passing a bowl of popcorn.) Say, I almost forgot. How about some for old time's sake?

(All the loggers help themselves; then the SIXTH LOGGER *goes on with his story.)*

SIXTH LOGGER

Paul always liked popcorn. I remember how he used to sit thinking and eating popcorn at night by the fire. And the harder he thought, the faster he ate. Used to eat up a couple of baskets full when he was thinking hard.

FIRST LOGGER

Well this time it all started with the popcorn blizzard. It was hot that summer and even the corn, which can take plenty of heat, was drying up on the stalks.

(The attention shifts to another part of the stage where PAUL *and the* FIRST LOGGER *are talking together and looking over a cornfield which is in the direction of the audience.)*

PAUL

Seems like even the corn is burning up this summer. Don't know what we'll feed the men if we lose this crop.

FIRST LOGGER

Look! Something's happening over there! The ears are beginning to burst!

PAUL

Where?

FIRST LOGGER

Over there! Watch out! It's exploding!

(The two duck as popcorn peppers the stage.)

PAUL

Looks like snow. If I wasn't so hot, I'd think it was a blizzard. I'm beginning to cool off just watching it.

FIRST LOGGER

The whole crop's popping. Do you suppose we can do anything with it?

PAUL

We'll see. That's an awful lot of corn to just let blow up. *(He picks up a kernel and tastes it thoughtfully.)* You know, it's not bad. *(Tastes another.)* Not bad at all. In fact, it's pretty good. Here, you eat some. Why not collect it in baskets and serve it up to the men?

FIRST LOGGER

(Tasting some.) It *is* good, only it's kind of hard to eat—one piece at a time. It would be easier if we could think of a way to hold a lot in our hands—

PAUL

I know! We can pour molasses over it so it sticks together. Ought to taste pretty good and it would be as easy to handle as bread.

FIRST LOGGER

(*Returning to his group.*) And that's what we did. From that day on there've been popcorn balls.

SECOND LOGGER

Sometimes I think Paul did more to change the ways of America than anyone else.

FOURTH LOGGER

And the map! Why, if I had time, I could tell you how he moved rivers and lakes!

FIFTH LOGGER

And dug Puget Sound!

SIXTH LOGGER

And made the Thousand Islands!

FIRST LOGGER

And started Old Faithful erupting!

SECOND LOGGER

And made the Pacific Ocean salty!

THIRD LOGGER

But we don't have time today. We'll have to save those stories for another night around the fire. But not one of us who knew him will ever forget them or the fact that Paul Bunyan was a giant.

STORYTELLER

Yes, Paul Bunyan *was* a giant. A big man who knew he was cut out for big things and he set out to do them.

(*The* STORYTELLER *goes off on one side and the group of* LOGGERS *go off on the other.*)

Nellie McCaslin

300

Bigger Than Life

Paul Bunyan and Slue-Foot Sue are characters from tall tales. Tall tale characters are often very big, bigger than any ordinary person. They can always do something better than anyone else.

If you were to tell a tall tale, who would be in it? Use the chart below to help you think of tall tale people. Maybe someone can hit more home runs than anyone else; you might call her Home Run Hazel. What do you think Menu Martin or Maxie Maps or Diamond Don does better than anyone else? What would be a name for a character who can run faster than anyone else? Or grow bigger apples?

What do I do better than anyone?	What is my name?
hit home runs	Home Run Hazel
?	Menu Martin
run faster	?
?	Maxie Maps
grow bigger apples	?
?	Diamond Don

Now try making up some of your own tall tale characters. Tell the group about them.

Molly
Mullett

by Patricia Coombs

303

Once upon a time, miles and years from here, lived Molly Mullett. She liked to climb trees and run races and jump over things.

Molly lived in a house with her mother and father. The house was in a village. It was a small village but it had a big problem. The big problem was a very large Ogre.

The Ogre was greedy and troublesome. Only the night before he had taken all the corn and pigs and gold he could carry. It was the second time in a month that he had robbed the village. He had also stolen some of the king's horses. Soon there would be no food or gold at all left in the village, and winter was coming.

In the Mullett house Molly took her father his slippers. Mr. Mullett wanted a son. Whenever he looked at Molly he said, "I do not need a sneezley, wheezley, sniveling girl. If I had a son like me he would make short work of that Ogre. He would be famous. And the village would be saved."

"I am not sneezley and wheezley and I do not snivel," said Molly.

Mr. Mullett whacked Molly for talking back.

"I always tell the truth," said Molly, "even when it hurts."

Out in the kitchen, Mrs. Mullett sighed. Mr. Mullett went back to his snoring.

307

Mrs. Mullett was always sweeping and weeping, cooking and looking, washing and wishing, frying and sighing, sitting and knitting.

Molly went to help Mrs. Mullett. Together they hung the wash. In the fields around them the crops were mashed and smashed by the Ogre's boots. Carts and wagons were overturned.

Molly took off her apron. "Mrs. Mullett," said Molly. "It is time for me to have an adventure. I have had enough of sweeping and weeping, frying and sighing, washing and wishing, cooking and looking."

"I don't think you should . . ." said Mrs. Mullett.

"Why?" asked Molly.

"I can't think why," said Mrs. Mullett, "but I'm sure . . ."

"Someone must take care of that Ogre," said Molly. "And no one else is doing it. So I will. The king has offered a reward. I will bring it home for you and Mr. Mullett. Mr. Mullett will see, once and for all, that I am not a wheezley, sneezley, sniveling person."

Mrs. Mullett fixed a bundle for Molly to take. She was still cooking, and looking out the window as Molly went away.

Molly walked and walked until she came to the king's castle. She said to the guard at the door, "I have come to see the king."

Molly waited and waited. At last she got to see the king.

"That troublesome Ogre has taken nearly all our food and gold," said Molly. "I am going to get it back. I may need some help getting across . . . ."

"Haw!" said the king. "You are a mere girl. A wheezley, measley, sneezley girl! Ten of my best soldiers have already been thrown back across Black Gulch by the Ogre. He smashed the bridge and gave them sprains and bruises and broken bones. He toasted and roasted their horses, saddles and all, and ate them for lunch. Go home. Stay indoors. The queen does a lot of sewing. You ought to try it."

"If you won't help me, I'll do it myself," said Molly. Out of the castle she marched and down the road.

311

Molly walked and walked and walked. It began to get dark. At last Molly came to bottomless Black Gulch. It was a long way across the gulch. But she could see a reddish glow and black smelly clouds from the Ogre's kitchen on the other side.

Molly sat on a stone to think. She opened her bundle to get something to eat while she thought.

As soon as she touched the bundle, a blackbird flew out of the shadows and landed beside her. Molly shared her sandwich with the blackbird.

"There must be a way I can get across," said Molly.

The blackbird pecked at something in the bottom of her bundle.

"A ball of yarn!" said Molly. "Whatever am I to do with that?"

The blackbird tugged at Molly's braid. Molly grinned. "A braid for a bridge!" Molly took the yarn and braided and braided and braided until she had a strip as long and as strong as a rope.

The blackbird took one end in his beak. He flew into the darkness over Black Gulch. When it was all unwound there was a tug at the other end. The blackbird flew back to Molly. Molly bent down and tied the yarn around a big stone.

Molly looked at the braid stretching across Black Gulch. "A bridge," said Molly, "but it will never hold me!"

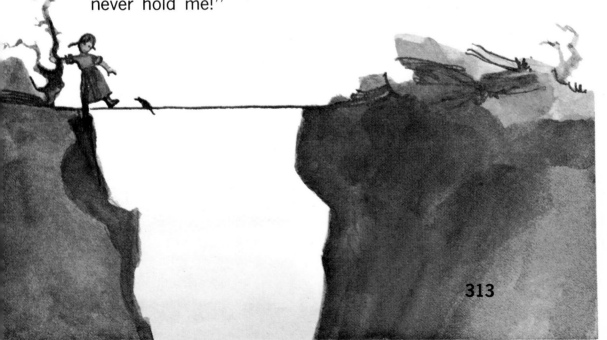

The blackbird bobbed his head. He flew to the bridge. He hopped out on it. Molly tried it with one foot. Then the other. It seemed as wide as a path, and with a grin she ran across Black Gulch. The blackbird flew beside her.

The glow from the Ogre's kitchen lit up the jagged rocks and scorched trees. Molly crept closer and closer. She looked in the window.

314

The Ogre was asleep in his chair. Dozens of plates and bowls and pots and pans were piled around him. The Ogre's wife was washing and drying stacks and stacks of dishes. A smaller Ogre was sitting on the floor. He was sniveling and driveling and bawling and squalling.

In one corner the stolen gold was heaped up and spilling from the sacks.

The blackbird tapped softly at the window. Molly pushed it open. The blackbird flew in. He flew at the small Ogre and gave him a pinch.

The small Ogre screamed so loudly that the Ogre woke up with an angry roar.

"I'm sorry, dear," said the Ogre's wife. She picked up the smaller Ogre and took him off to bed.

The Ogre stomped around the kitchen. He picked up two pies and a cake and ate them in

three gulps. He was about to eat another pie when the blackbird landed on it. The Ogre made a grab for the bird. The bird flew to a corner. With a roar the Ogre chased the blackbird around and around and around. There were so many dishes and pots and pans on the floor that the Ogre stumbled. One foot got stuck in a pot and the Ogre went sprawling.

Molly saw her chance. She slipped through the window and raced to the corner where the sacks of gold were piled.

"It's a good thing I'm strong," said Molly. She heaved a sack of gold over her shoulder. Just as she got to the window the Ogre sat up. He saw her. Out the window went Molly with the sack of gold, the blackbird right behind her.

Into the darkness they went, back toward Black Gulch. The Ogre came roaring after them. The iron pot sounded like thunder as the Ogre came stumbling over the rocks. Molly was quick as well as strong. She zigged and she zagged and she ducked and dodged, and the iron pot slowed the Ogre down enough for Molly to keep ahead, just out of reach.

Molly got to the bridge. She raced across. Behind her, the blackbird flew at the Ogre's head. He pecked at his ears and tweaked his beard. By the time the Ogre got to the gulch, Molly was on the other side. The blackbird flew back to Molly, the yarn in his beak. She rolled up the yarn and hid it under a stone. The blackbird showed her the way home in the dark.

Behind them they could hear the Ogre rumbling and grumbling and roaring, the iron pot banging over the stones.

"Well done, blackbird," said Molly. "Thank you." She took a cookie from her bundle and crumbled it in her hand for him to eat.

By the time the moon went down, Molly was home and asleep in her bed, the sack of gold beside her. The blackbird had flown away.

319

In the morning Molly showed Mrs. Mullett and Mr. Mullett the gold.

"I got it back from the Ogre last night," said Molly.

Mr. Mullett rubbed his eyes and blinked.

"Now I will take it to the king," said Molly. "We will get a reward and the village will have some gold to buy food."

"Wait," said Mr. Mullett. He put on his best clothes. He shaved. He took the sack of gold and he and Molly went to see the king.

The king beamed. "Thank you, Mullett," said the king. "You have done what ten of my best soldiers could not do. You are strong and brave."

"Oh, no, King, sir," said Mr. Mullett. "Molly here, she was the one."

"Ah, Mullett," cried the king, "you are as gallant as you are brave."

"But Molly, she . . ." said Mr. Mullett.

"Foolishness! Nonsense! Haw!" cried the king. "A mere girl, a measley, wheezley, sneezley girl outwit the Ogre! Haw!"

And the king gave Mr. Mullett the reward and said, "The whole kingdom thanks you, Mullett, for your courage and bravery."

Mr. Mullett turned very red and mumbled, "Thank you, King, sir."

Molly shrugged and grinned. She knew the truth, even if the king didn't. And it was her adventure, not Mr. Mullett's, or the king's, or anybody else's.

321

Meanwhile, the Ogre had gotten his foot out of the cooking pot and he was angry. One night, back he came across Black Gulch, swinging his sword and roaring. He squashed houses and barns, smashed the rest of the fields into mud, and knocked down part of the castle walls.

The king was cross about the castle. He called in the Royal Seer. Then the king went to see Mr. Mullett.

"See here, Mullett," said the king. "You'll have to get rid of the Ogre altogether. Getting the gold back is not enough. The Royal Seer thinks it is the Ogre's sword that gives him his great strength. Without the sword he is merely a roaring, boring oaf. He very likely keeps the sword under his pillow while he sleeps. All you have to do is get the sword away from him. Then he won't bother us anymore."

"ME? The Ogre's *sword?*" Mr. Mullett choked on his pipe. "I can't do that! That's very dangerous and . . ."

"Haw! Nonsense, my good fellow! You're too modest. I am *ordering* you to do it. If you aren't at the castle tomorrow with the sword, Mullett, it's the dungeon for you."

The king rode away. Mr. Mullett went to lie down and rest. He did not feel very well.

"Mrs. Mullett," said Molly, "it is time for another adventure."

Mrs. Mullett fixed Molly a bundle to take with her. Still cooking and looking, she watched Molly walking down the path.

By the time it began to get dark, Molly was climbing among the rocks at the edge of Black Gulch. She found where she'd hidden the yarn. As soon as she touched it, the blackbird flew from the shadows and landed beside her. Molly sat down and opened her bundle. She shared her sandwich with the blackbird.

"This is an even bigger adventure than the first," said Molly. "I'm glad I'm not afraid of being scared. Mr. Mullett would be most unhappy if the king put him in a dungeon."

They finished eating and the blackbird pecked at something in the bottom of the bundle. Molly looked. It was a small pair of scissors.

"What shall I do with these against the Ogre's sword?" said Molly.

The blackbird pecked at her pocket. Molly grinned and shrugged. She put the scissors in her pocket. As he had before, the blackbird took the braided yarn in his beak and flew over Black Gulch and back again to Molly.

Molly ran quickly across the strip of bridge. The glow from the Ogre's kitchen shone bright as a red angry moon.

Molly looked in the window. The Ogre's wife was just taking the screaming small Ogre off to bed. The Ogre was in his chair.

The blackbird tapped at the window. Molly opened it. The blackbird flew inside. He tweaked the Ogre's hair. The Ogre roared and leaped to his feet.

The blackbird pinched the Ogre's ears until they bled. The Ogre grabbed for him. Around and around and around they went, the Ogre roaring and reaching. Around the kitchen and down the hall they went.

325

Molly saw her chance. Quick as a minnow, she slipped inside and hid herself among the sacks of gold.

Seconds later the Ogre came howling and scowling back again. He swung his sword at the blackbird and chopped off a few tail feathers just as the blackbird flew out the window. The Ogre slammed the window shut.

"Dratted bird," growled the Ogre. He stomped over and had a few blackbird pies and two gallons of pig stew for a snack.

The Ogre's wife trudged back to the kitchen to wash more dishes and pots and pans. As she reached for a towel, she screeched: "EEEE! A mouse! A mouse!"

"Where?" roared the Ogre.

"There!" The Ogre's wife pointed to where Molly was hidden among the sacks of gold.

Before Molly could think or blink, the Ogre's hand lifted her into the air.

"Well, well, a village mouse! A gold-stealing mouse come back for more. A measley, sneezley, wheezley mouse, ah ha! oh ho! ho ha!" laughed the Ogre with his terrible smelly laugh.

326

327

"Quick, a sack for this mouse, wife! Tomorrow I will fix it a cage and it will be a pet for our Ogrelet. We can watch him squeeze and pinch it!"

The Ogre stuffed Molly into a sack and tied a big knot at the top. He dropped it at his feet and yawned.

"I'll sleep well tonight," roared the Ogre. He patted his belly and belched his terrible belch. Off to bed went the Ogre and his wife. Before long their huge snores shook the walls and rattled the pots and pans.

Molly fought to get out of the sack. She kicked and pushed and shoved with all her might. No matter how hard she tried, the knot held fast. Molly stopped kicking.

"I just have to think my way out of this," Molly said to herself. Then she remembered. "The scissors! I forgot about the scissors!"

Molly took the scissors out of her pocket. With a snippety-snip-snick she cut a hole in the sack and slipped out. She ran to the window and opened it for the blackbird.

With the blackbird on her shoulder, she tiptoed down the long, long dark hall to the Ogre's room.

The Ogre's snores were deafening. And they smelled terrible. Molly crept up beside the Ogre's bed. A gleam of moonlight shone on the handle of the sword sticking out from under the Ogre's pillow.

Molly grabbed the handle of the sword. She pulled it from under the pillow and the Ogre's snoring head.

In a flash Molly was out of the room, down the hall, across the kitchen and out the window, the blackbird right beside her. Between the rocks and trees they ran. They had not gone far when there was a terrible roar behind them. The Ogre, awakened by his own snores, had found his sword gone and the sack empty.

Molly ran faster than she'd ever run before. She and the blackbird were over the bridge and had it rolled up as the Ogre got to the gulch. The Ogre roared and howled and yowled. All at once there were other sounds. The sounds of trees being pulled up by the roots and thrown across the gulch.

"I think the Royal Seer was wrong about the Ogre's sword," said Molly. "He's making a bridge! He's as strong as ever, and here he comes!"

330

The Ogre strode across. Molly swung the Ogre's sword at the Ogre's shins. He howled a terrible howl. The sword was very sharp and Molly's aim was very good.

Another swing of the sword and the Ogre lost his balance. Down, down, down into bottomless Black Gulch tumbled the Ogre. Rocks and trees tumbled down with him.

The sound of hooves came from the darkness behind Molly. The king and his soldiers, hearing roars and crashes and sounds of battle, had come to help.

The king got down from his horse. "Where's Mullett?" he cried. "Dear me, the Ogre must have swallowed him before he fell into the gulch."

"Nonsense," said Molly, "I'm the only Mullett here." She leaned on the Ogre's sword to catch her breath. "Mr. Mullett has no taste for adventure. Doubtless he is in bed, dreaming of breakfast."

The Ogre's roars echoed from deep in the gulch, then faded to silence.

The king knelt at Molly's feet. "You have saved us all from the Ogre's power. You are the strongest and bravest person in the kingdom. Whatever you want that I can grant, you shall have."

Molly shrugged and grinned and thanked the king. "I just want to have adventures. I can find them myself, with the blackbird's help."

The king knighted Molly then and there. He rode her home on his Royal Horse, the blackbird on her shoulder. On the way, Molly told the king the tale of her adventures with the blackbird and the Ogre.

"Henceforth," said the king, "the blackbird will be the Royal Bird of our kingdom, and you, Molly Mullett, will be our Very Most Royal Knight."

The king rode up to the door of Molly's house and helped her down from the horse.

Mr. Mullett crawled out of bed and peered out the door. "The king is here! Tell him I'm sick!"

"Molly's home," said Mrs. Mullett. "And she has the Ogre's sword."

The next day everyone in the village helped build a bridge across Black Gulch. Then they took their carts and baskets and wagons and brought back everything the Ogre had stolen from them. Everything he hadn't eaten. The Ogre's wife and the small Ogre had run far away.

Not long after that, Mrs. Mullett had a son. Mr. Mullett made a great fuss over him. "At last, all my dreams will come true!" said Mr. Mullett.

When the baby cried, Mr. Mullett waved the Ogre's sword and told him to be brave. The baby yelled louder.

Molly shrugged and grinned and picked up the baby. "Mr. Mullett," she said, "I do not think you'll ever learn."

Mr. Mullett didn't whack her. He sighed. Molly always told the truth, when it hurt and when it didn't.

"Mrs. Mullett," said Molly, "why did you put the ball of yarn and the scissors into my bundle?"

Mrs. Mullett sat quietly sewing and knowing. She simply smiled.

Molly gave her a kiss and put down the baby. Then she went to play baseball with the king and the other knights.

337

Key to Pronunciation

Letter Symbol for a sound	Key Word and Its Respelling	Letter Symbol for a sound	Key Word and Its Respelling
a	pat (PAT)	ch	church (CHERCH)
ah	far (FAHR)	hw	when (HWEN)
ai	air (AIR)	ks	mix (MIKS)
aw	jaw (JAW)	kw	quick (KWIK)
ay	pay (PAY)	ng	thing (THING)
e	pet (PET)		finger (FING-gər)
ee	bee (BEE)	sh	shoe (SHOO)
ehr	berry (BEHR-ee)	ss	case (KAYSS)
er	term (TERM)	th	thing (THING)
i	pit (PIT)	<u>th</u>	this (<u>TH</u>IS)
igh	sigh (SIGH)	zh	pleasure (PLEZH-ər)
ihr	pier (PIHR)		
o	pot (POT)		
oh	oh, boat (BOHT)		
oi	oil (OIL)		
oo	boot, rule (ROOL)		
or	for (FOR)		
ow	power (POW-ər)		
u	put, book (BUK)		
uh	cut (KUHT)		

y	used in place of (igh) before two consonant letters as in child (CHYLD)
ə	represents the sound for any vowel spelling when a syllable is sounded very weakly, as in the first syllable of *about*, or the last syllables of *item*, *gallop*, or *focus*, or the middle syllable of *charity*

Glossary

ad An advertisement. A public notice telling about the good qualities of something for sale: If you look in the newspaper, you may find an *ad* for the kind of dog you want.

ad·mit (ad-MIT) 1. To let someone enter: I cannot *admit* you without a ticket. 2. To confess: Joe *admits* that he is afraid to go into the old house. **admitted, admitting.**

af·fect (ə-FEKT) 1. To bring about a change in: Rainfall *affects* the growth of plants. 2. To arouse emotion: Sad movies *affect* me. **affected, affecting.**

al·li·ga·tor (AL-ə-gay-tər) A large reptile with a broad nose, long tail, scaly hide, and sharp teeth: *Alligators* live in swamps and rivers of southeastern United States.

The pronunciation system and word entries are adapted from *The Ginn Intermediate Dictionary,* © Copyright, 1977, 1974, 1973, by Xerox Corporation, published by Ginn and Company (Xerox Corporation).

al·lo·sau·rus (al-ə-SAWR-uhss) A dinosaur; a meat-eating reptile of long ago.

ant·ler (ANT-lər) One of two large branched horns on the head of an animal of the deer family.

ar·mor (AHR-mər) 1. Any safe covering: The turtle carries a shell of *armor*. 2. A metal covering. like a suit, worn for protection in battle. **armored, armoring.**

as·sem·bly (ə-SEM-blee) 1. A gathering together: The *assembly* of the troops took just two minutes. 2. A gathering or meeting of people for a common purpose: Today's student *assembly* will be a football rally. **assemblies.**

a·ston·ish (ə-STON-ish) To fill with wonder: It would *astonish* me if we won first prize. **astonished, astonishing.**

a·stray (ə-STRAY) 1. Not in the right place or direction: The camper wandered *astray* when he lost his compass. 2. Away from proper behavior: Dennis went *astray* because of a bad temper.

bad·ger (BAJ-ər) 1. A short-legged, furry animal that lives in a hole in the ground. 2. To pester or bother: Don't *badger* me while I work. **badgered, badgering.**

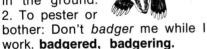

bait (BAYT) 1. Food placed on a hook or trap to catch fish and other animals. 2. Something used to trick a person: The money was left on the table as *bait* to catch the thief. 3. To place food on a hook or in a trap: Please *bait* my hook with a

worm. 4. To tease: I saw Kit *bait* the old dog by holding up a bone. **baited, baiting.**

ban·quet (BANG-kwit) A feast in honor of a person, group, or special day.

bare·back (BAIR-bak) On a horse's bare back without a saddle: Riding *bareback* is not easy.

bar·gain (BAHR-gin) 1. An agreement made for a purchase, trade, or service: Mom made a *bargain* with the owner to buy the automobile. 2. Something that can be bought at less than the usual price. 3. To make an agreement for a purchase, trade, or service. **bargained, bargaining.**

bass (BASS) A kind of fish found in either fresh or salt water. **bass** or **basses.**

ba·ton (bə-TON) A stick or rod used by a conductor or leader to direct an orchestra or band.

bay 1. An inlet of a body of water. 2. A deep bark: The hunter heard the *bay* of the dog. 3. A reddish-brown color. 4. To bark: Have you ever heard a wolf *bay* at the moon? **bayed, baying.**

beam (BEEM) 1. A large, strong piece of wood or metal used to hold up a building. 2. A stream of light. 3. The greatest width of a ship. 4. To smile: My little sister *beams* whenever I give her a new toy. **beamed, beaming.**

bel·low (BEL-oh) 1. To make a loud, deep sound or outcry: He began to *bellow* orders to the crew. 2. A loud, deep shout: The giant cried out in a deep *bellow*. **bellowed, bellowing.**

bleat (BLEET) 1. The noise or cry made by sheep or goats, or a

sound like it: the *bleat* of a goat.
2. To make the noise or cry made
by sheep or goats: The goat *bleats*
loudly. **bleated, bleating.**

bliz·zard (BLIZ-ərd)   A heavy
snowstorm with strong, cold winds.

blur (BLER)   1. To smear: Rain will
blur your ink drawing.   2. To make
unclear in outline: If you move the
camera, the picture will *blur*.   3. To
darken or dim: We watched the
fog *blur* the lighthouse beam.
4. A smear or blot: The car was
going so fast that all we saw was
a *blur.* **blurred, blurring.**

bon·bon (BON-bon)   A piece of
candy, usually soft with a fancy
shape.

boo·ty (BOO-tee)   Goods stolen by
an armed force: The pirates set
fire to the town after they had
searched the houses for *booty.*

bound·a·ry (BOWN-dree or BOWN-
də-ree)   A line that limits or
separates: The Rio Grande forms
part of the *boundary* between
Mexico and the United States.
boundaries.

brim   1. The top rim of a container:
The glass was filled to the
brim.   2. The outer rim of a hat:
The children turned up the *brims*
of their hats.

bron·to·saur·us (brahn-tə-SAWR-uhss)
A huge dinosaur that lived long
ago in North America.

broth   1. A soup made from water
in which meat, chicken, and/or
vegetables have been boiled.
2. The water in which meat or
vegetables have been boiled.

buck (BUHK)   1. A male animal,
especially a deer.   2. To rear suddenly: The horse will *buck* until the

rider falls off.   3. To oppose; go
against. **bucked, bucking.**

buck·eye
(BUHK-igh)
1. A tree be-
longing to the
horse chest-
nut family with showy bunches
of small flowers, large leaves,
and large brown seeds.   2. The
large brown seeds from the
tree.

calf (KAF)   1. A young cow or
bull.   2. The soft leather that
comes from a young cow or
bull.   3. The back part of the leg
between the knee and the ankle.
calves (KAVZ).

chat   1. A relaxed talk: I had a nice
chat with Mrs. Smith yesterday.
2. To talk in a relaxed way: Jack
wants to *chat* with you before
class. **chatted, chatting.**

chuck·le (CHUHK-əl)   To laugh
softly; laugh to oneself. A low
laugh. **chuckled, chuckling.**

cli·mate (KLIGH-mit)   1. The usual
weather conditions of an area:
Polar bears live in very cold
climates.   2. An atmosphere or
general feeling: a *climate* of joy.
climates.

comb (KOHM)   1. A short thin piece
of metal or plastic with a row of
teeth used to fix or clean the hair.
2. A crest on the head of a
rooster or other bird.   3. To
untangle or fix with a comb.   4. To
search or look for thoroughly:
Doris *combed* the library looking
for the right book. **combed,
combing.**

con·crete (KON-kreet)   1. A mixture
of cement with water and sand or

gravel used for building: That tall building is made of *concrete*. 2. (kon-KREET) Solid, real.

con·duc·tor (kən-DUHK-tər) 1. A person who collects money or sells tickets on trains, buses, and so on. 2. A person who leads a band. 3. Something that carries or sends electricity, sound, or heat: Metal is a good *conductor* of heat.

con·tin·ue (kən-TIN-yoo) To go on; keep doing: Please *continue* reading for as long as you want to. **continued, continuing.**

cor·ner (KOR-nər) 1. The spot where two streets or sidewalks meet: The group will meet at the *corner* of Main and First Streets at ten o'clock. 2. The place where two surfaces or lines come together: Chairs were placed in each *corner* of the room. 3. A faraway place: Many people have explored all *corners* of the Earth. 4. To force into a place from which there is no getting away: If the police can *corner* the robber, they can catch him. **cornered, cornering.**

cot (KOT) A lightweight, narrow bed.

coup·le (KUHP-əl) 1. Two together; a pair: Form a line in *couples*. 2. To join together: We watched the engine *couple* with the freight cars. 3. To pair off: *Couple* yourselves with someone who has the same number as you. **coupled, coupling.**

cray·fish (KRAY-fish) Also **crawfish** 1. A fish that is like a lobster but smaller in size. 2. A small, spiny lobster.

creek (KREEK or KRIK) 1. A path of water smaller than a river; a stream. 2. An inlet or bay of small size.

croc·o·dile (KROK-ə-dighl) A large lizard-like reptile with a thick-skinned body, long powerful tail, and long-pointed nose. **crocodiles.**

cross (KRAWSS) In a bad mood; angry. **crossly.**

dell (DEL) A small valley.

de·tec·tive (di-TEK-tiv) 1. One whose job it is to find secret facts or solve crimes, often working with or for the police. 2. One who gets information that is not easy to find. **detectives.**

dim 1. Not bright: The light was so *dim* that we could hardly see each other. 2. Not clear: She has a *dim* memory of her childhood. 3. To make less bright: *Dim* the lights so we can see the movie. **dimmer, dimmest, dimmed, dimming, dimly.**

di·no·saur (DIGH-nə-sor) One of the class of long-tailed reptiles that lived millions of years ago.

drum (DRUHM) A hollow musical instrument covered with a thin layer of skin on one or both ends and played by beating with sticks or with both hands.

earn (ERN) 1. To gain (pay) for one's work. 2. To win or deserve (through effort): Jane *earned* praise for her good report card. **earned, earning.**

e·rupt (ih-RUHPT) To break out or burst forth as lava and hot ash do from a volcano. **erupted, erupting.**

ev·er·green (EV-ər-green) A tree, shrub, or other plant that stays green all through the year.

341

fate (FAYT) 1. What some people believe causes things to happen: John believed *fate* would bring him much money, but Bill believed in hard work. 2. An outcome that cannot be helped: It was Joan's *fate* to be chosen the leader.

fid·dle (FID-l) 1. A violin. 2. To play a violin. 3. To act in a restless way. 4. To make a certain noise: A cricket was *fiddling* in the garden. **fiddled, fiddling.**

fin 1. A thin, winglike or bladelike part of the body of a fish or certain other animals. 2. Any part that is like the fin of a fish: The rocket's *fins* keep it moving straight.

firm (FERM) 1. Solid; not easily moved, crushed, or divided: The fresh melons have a *firm* rind. 2. Positive; strong: *firm* opinion. 3. A business company. **firmer, firmest, firmly.**

flinch 1. To shrink away from what is dangerous, frightening, difficult, or the like. 2. To twitch with pain or in fear of pain; wince. **flinched, flinching.**

flip·per (FLIP-ər) 1. A flat, broad fin used for swimming by animals such as seals and whales. 2. (Usually plural) Rubber devices for the feet in the shape of fins, used for swimming.

fos·sil (FOSS-l) The remains or imprint of a plant or animal.

frame (FRAYM) 1. The enclosing edge of a picture, door, or window. 2. The parts of a building that hold everything up or together: the *frame* of a house. 3. The (human) body; skeleton. 4. To make a frame. 5. To put a frame on or

around: *frame* a picture. **framed, framing.**

fren·zy (FREN-zee) Wild mental excitement usually leading to feverish activity; brief loss of reason and control; unusual excitement. **frenzies, frenzied.**

ghost (GOHST) The spirit of a dead person that, it is believed by some, is able to appear or to haunt the living.

gill (GIL) The part of the body that permits fish and other animals to breathe in water.

glance (GLANSS) 1. A fast look: Shirley was in a hurry and had only a *glance* at the parade. 2. To take a fast look: I saw him *glance* at me and then turn away. **glanced, glancing, glances.**

glum (GLUHM) Not happy; sad: Pat is *glum* because the game was called off.

gnash (NASH) To grind (the teeth) together: Do you *gnash* your teeth at night? **gnashed, gnashing.**

gob·ble (GOB-əl) 1. To eat very fast: You should not *gobble* your food so fast. 2. To make a noise like a turkey. **gobbled, gobbling.**

grav·el (GRAV-əl) Small pieces of stone: Many walks and roads are made with *gravel.*

han·dle (HAN-dl) 1. That part of an object to be held or turned. 2. To touch, move, or hold with the hands: *Handle* the kitten gently. 3. To manage or control. **handled, handling, handles.**

her·mit (HER-mit) 1. A person who chooses to live alone. 2. A spiced cookie made with molasses.

hob·ble (HOB-əl) 1. To walk with a limp. 2. A limping walk. **hobbled, hobbling.**

hull (HUHL) 1. The main part of the body of a ship. 2. The outer covering of a seed, fruit, or nut. 3. To remove the covering of a seed or fruit. **hulled, hulling.**

i·dle (IGHD-l) 1. Not working or active: *Idle* hands make mischief. 2. Lazy or unwilling to work: The *idle* girl wouldn't help with the chores.

il·lu·sion (ih-LOO-zhən) 1. An appearance that seems to be real, but is not. 2. A false belief.

knap·sack (NAP-sak) A bag or pack made of heavy cloth for carrying things on the back: We can carry sleeping bags in our *knapsack.*

lab·o·ra·to·ry (LAB-ə-rə-tor-ee) A room or building used for scientific work. **laboratories.**

la·dle (LAYD-l) 1. A spoon with a long handle and large bowl, used for serving 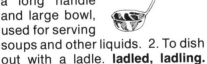 soups and other liquids. 2. To dish out with a ladle. **ladled, ladling.**

lamp·post (LAMP-pohst) A post that holds a street lamp.

las·so (LASS-oh) 1. A long rope with a slip knot that forms a loop at one end, used for catching cattle or horses. 2. To catch with a lasso. **lassos** or **lassoes, lassoed, lassoing.**

lest For fear that: Be quiet *lest* you wake the children.

log·ger (LAW-gər) 1. Someone who cuts down trees. 2. A machine that loads logs.

lug (LUHG) To drag or pull with much trouble: Joe had to *lug* the heavy suitcase up the steps. **lugged, lugging.**

lull·a·by (LUHL-ə-bigh) A quiet song to put a baby to sleep. **lullabies.**

lum·ber (LUHM-bər) 1. Sawed logs ready for use; boards. 2. To move in a noisy or clumsy way: Bears sometimes *lumber* through the woods. **lumbered, lumbering.**

mac·a·ro·ni (mak-ə-ROH-nee) A food made of wheat flour paste that is formed into various shapes, dried, and boiled before being eaten.

ma·ple (MAY-pəl) 1. A shade tree, one type of which produces the sap used in making maple syrup. 2. The wood of the maple tree. **maples.**

mer·maid (MER-mayd) In fairy tales, a creature with the head and upper body of a woman, but the lower body of a fish.

min·i·a·ture (MIN-ee-ə-chur or MIN-ə-chur) 1. A very small painting or portrait. 2. A tiny copy of anything: I have a *miniature* racing car. **miniatures.**

min·now (MIN-oh) A small freshwater fish.

mod·est (MOD-ist) 1. Shy; bashful. 2. Not showy in one's dress or behavior; She is *modest* about her work. **modestly.**

moon·beam (MOON-beem) A stream of moonlight.

mums (MUHMZ) Chrysanthemums. A large flower or the plant on which it grows: Some *mums* are yellow and some are white.

mus·tang (MUHSS-tang) A wild horse of the plains of North America.

nail (NAYL) 1. A hard, slender piece of pointed metal used to hold together materials such as wood. 2. A fingernail or toenail. 3. To hold together with a nail or nails: We can *nail* the picture on the wall. **nailed, nailing.**

nei·ther (NEE-thər or NIGH-thər) 1. Not either: *Neither* shoe is wet. 2. Not either one: *Neither* of us likes baseball. 3. Nor: Dad doesn't smoke; *neither* does Mother.

nib·ble (NIB-əl) 1. To eat or chew with quick, small bites. 2. To eat small bits slowly: We always *nibble* popcorn at the movies. 3. A small bite; quick small bites. **nibbled, nibbling, nibbles.**

nug·get (NUHG-it) 1. A small lump: a *nugget* of gold. 2. A small, valuable part: a *nugget* of information.

oar·lock (OR-lock) An object, often u-shaped, on the side of a boat to hold the oar in place. **oarlocks.**

or·di·nary (ORD-n-ehr-ee) 1. Usual: My *ordinary* bedtime is nine o'clock. 2. Common, not special.

os·trich (OSS-trich or AWSS-trich) A large, long-legged bird that cannot fly, often found in Asia and Africa where it is dry: An *ostrich* can run fast because of its powerful legs. **ostriches.**

pad·dle (PAD-l) 1. A short pole with a broad blade, used with both hands to move a boat through the water. 2. Anything shaped like this, often used for striking or beating: Ping-Pong *paddle*. 3. To move through water with a paddle or with a paddle-like motion. 4. To move about (in the water) by moving the hands and feet quickly. **paddled, paddling, paddles.**

pa·le·on·tol·o·gist (pay-lee-on-TOL-ə-jist) A person who studies fossils and very old forms of life.

pars·ley (PAHRSS-lee) A plant with small bright green curly leaves, often used to flavor food.

pep·per (PEP-ər) 1. The small berry of a vine used ground or whole as a sharp flavoring in food. 2. A bell-shaped food tasting anywhere from mild to hot and differing in color from red to green. 3. To sprinkle with pepper. 4. To hit rapidly with small objects. **peppered, peppering.**

per·cus·sion (pər-KUHSH-ən) 1. The hitting of one thing against another. 2. A group of musical instruments, such as drums or

344

piano, whose tone is produced by hitting or striking.

piece (PEESS) 1. A scrap, bit, or chunk; one of the parts that make up a thing: The dish fell and broke into a hundred *pieces.* 2. A creative work, such as a play, statue, painting, or musical composition: *pieces* of music.

pet·ri·fy (PET-rə-figh) 1. To turn into stone. 2. To stun with fear or some other strong feelings: Jill *petrifies* her friends with ghost stories. **petrified, petrifying.**

pier (PIHR) A structure built on posts out over water and used as a dock or a walk.

plas·ter (PLASS-tər) 1. A thick, sticky mixture which is spread on walls and ceilings where it dries to a hard surface. 2. To cover with plaster; to spread (anything) as if using plaster. 3. To cover fully or widely: Let's *plaster* the wall with pictures. **plastered, plastering.**

plat·form (PLAT-form) 1. A flat structure, like a stage or stand, that is raised above the area around it. 2. A formal statement of the beliefs or plans of an official, political party, or other group.

plow 1. A tool or device, usually pulled by a tractor or horse, used to cut into and turn over soil. 2. A device used for pushing or lifting quantities, as of snow or earth.

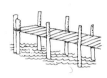

plunge (PLUNJ) 1. To dive or rush into: *Plunge* into the pool. 2. To push something quickly into: The cook *plunges* the lobster into hot water. 3. To rush forward or downward: We watched the car *plunge* down the steep hill. 4. A dive or sudden push forward or downward: We went for a *plunge* in the pool. **plunged, plunging.**

pod A shell that holds the seeds of a plant: *peapod.*

pol·ish (POL-ish) 1. To make or become smooth and shiny: *Polish* the floor. 2. To make better or finish: *Polish* a report. 3. That which is used to make something smooth and shiny: shoe *polish.* 4. Shininess: the *polish* of silver. **polished, polishing, polishes.**

pre·tend (pri-TEND) 1. To make (something or oneself) appear to be what (it or one) isn't. 2. To make believe. 3. A make-believe object: He rode the *pretend* horse at the supermarket. **pretended, pretending.**

pride (PRIGHD) 1. A self-satisfied feeling because of a deed, accomplishment, or possession. 2. Something that causes good or self-satisfied feelings: Beth's hair is her *pride.* 3. Conceit, being too pleased with oneself. 4. To feel good or self-satisfied about.

prog·ress (PROG-ress) 1. Improvement; forward movement; growth. (prə-GRESS) 2. To go forward; move ahead; show improvement. **progressed, progressing.**

pro·tect (prə-TEKT) To defend against harm or damage; guard;

shelter: Helmets *protect* heads. **protected, protecting.**

pry (PRIGH) 1. To lift or move by using a lever. 2. To snoop; search for information. **pried, prying.**

quiv·er (KWIV-ər) 1. To shake or bring about a slight shaking; tremble: His lower lip began to *quiver* when he heard the sad news. 2. A slight shaking. 3. A case used to hold arrows. **quivered, quivering.**

rare (RAIR) 1. Not often found; unusual: a *rare* illness. 2. Very special: a *rare* skill. 3. Very thin, as air: The air was *rare* at the top of the mountain. 4. Not well-cooked: Do you like your beef *rare?* **rarer, rarest, rarely.**

rear (RIHR) 1. The back part: the *rear* of a bus. 2. Of or at the back: the *rear* door. 3. To rise on hind legs: The horse started to *rear* in fright. **reared, rearing.**

rec·i·pe (RESS-ə-pee) A set of directions for preparing anything, especially food. **recipes.**

reel A wheel or spool used for winding film, thread, rope, yarn, or other materials.

re·late (ri-LAYT) 1. To associate or connect two or more things or people: Everyone in a family is *related.* 2. To tell: *relate* a story. **related, relating.**

rep·tile (REP-til or REP-tighl) A cold-blooded animal that has a backbone and moves by creeping or crawling: Snakes, lizards, turtles, and alligators are *reptiles.*

re·spon·si·bil·i·ty (ri-spon-sə-BIL-ə-tee) 1. The state of being responsible: Chris accepted the *responsibility* of caring for her dog. 2. A person or thing for which someone is responsible.

re·spon·si·ble (ri-SPON-sə-bəl) 1. Having a duty toward something: Parents are *responsible* for raising their children. 2. Being the cause of: The broken machine was *responsible* for the loud noise. 3. Having many things that must be done: a *responsible* job. 4. Able to accept duties; worthy of trust: The most *responsible* worker will get the job. **responsibly.**

ri·dic·u·lous (ri-DIK-yə-ləss) Very silly; making no sense; absurd: We laughed at the clown's *ridiculous* behavior. **ridiculously.**

rip·ple (RIP-əl) 1. A very small wave: The rain caused *ripples* to appear on the pond. 2. To make very small waves: The breeze *ripples* the surface of the pond. **rippled, rippling, ripples.**

route (ROOT or ROWT) 1. The road or way to go. 2. A way that follows a usual pattern or is made up of actions at a series of places: newspaper *route.* 3. To send along the usual road or way: We will *route* you the shortest way. **routed, routing, routes.**

rus·set (RUHSS-ət) 1. Yellowish-brown; reddish-brown. 2. A rough russet-colored cloth. 3. A kind of apple with a brownish skin.

scale (SKAYL) 1. One of the many hard, flat plates that cover certain animals, especially reptiles and fish. 2. An object used for weighing. 3. Eight notes in music that follow one another. 4. To climb: *Scale* a ladder. 5. To remove scales from: You can *scale* a fish before you cook it. **scaled, scaling, scales.**

scut·tle (SKUHT-l) To run with quick movements; to scamper. **scuttled, scuttling.**

sep·a·rate (SEP-ə-rayt) 1. To keep apart by putting something between: Draw a line to *separate* your side from mine. 2. To put into different groups: We can *separate* the red jellybeans from the green ones. 3. To part: We are never going to find him if we do not *separate.* 4. (SEP-ə-rit) Not joined; not shared; apart: The garage is *separate* from the house. **separated, separating, separately.**

shab·by (SHAB-ee) 1. Worn-out: This coat is so *shabby* that I can't wear it anymore. 2. Wearing old, worn clothing: a *shabby* tramp. **shabbier, shabbiest, shabbily.**

shade (SHAYD) 1. The darkness brought about when an object cuts off the light from the sun or anything else: the *shade* of a tree. 2. An object used to block or cut off the light: a window *shade.* 3. How light or dark a color is: many *shades* of green. 4. To block from light: *Shade* yourself from the sun, or you might get a bad sunburn. **shaded, shading.**

shal·low (SHAL-oh) 1. Not deep: a *shallow* stream. 2. Not deep or careful (in thought): Because he does not think carefully, people say he is a *shallow* person.

sheep·herders Those who gather, move, or take care of large numbers of sheep.

shoe·shine (SHOO-SHIGHN) Having to do with the shining of shoes.

shrink (SHRINGK) 1. To make or become smaller or less: Did the sweater *shrink* when you washed it? 2. To draw back; shy away (from): *shrink* from a dog. **shrank** or **shrunk, shrunk** or **shrunken, shrinking.**

shrub (SHRUHB) A woody plant that has many stems beginning at its base; a bush.

shrug (SHRUHG) 1. To raise the shoulders for a short moment, as if to show uncertainty or no interest. 2. The motion of raising the shoulders for a short moment: She gave a *shrug* when I asked her if she wanted to go to the game. **shrugged, shrugging.**

shud·der (SHUHD-ər) 1. To shake suddenly: I began to *shudder* when I heard a noise outside. 2. A sudden shaking. **shuddered, shuddering.**

sim·mer (SIM-ər) 1. To boil gently. 2. To cook just at the boiling point.

sire (SIGHR) 1. A father or grandfather. 2. A four-legged animal's father. **sires.**

skel·e·ton (SKEL-ə-tən) 1. The bones as the framework of a body. 2. A framework or outline of something. **skeletal.**

slith·er (SLITH-ər) To move in a sliding, slipping, or gliding motion: Did you see the snake *slither* in the grass? **slithered, slithering.**

sly (SLIGH) 1. Smart; able to fool others. 2. Secret; sneaky: The robber was very *sly*. **slier** or **slyer, sliest** or **slyest, slyly, slyness.**

snare drum A small drum with strings across the bottom side.

snif·fle (SNIF-l) To sniff over and over, as when one is crying or has a cold. **sniffled, sniffling.**

snooze (SNOOZ) 1. To take a nap; to sleep. 2. A nap. **snoozed, snoozing.**

snort 1. To force air through the nose with a sudden loud sound to show surprise, dislike, or anger: Can you *snort* like a bull? 2. The act or sound of snorting: The bull gave an angry *snort* and then charged. **snorted, snorting.**

soothe (SOOTH) 1. To calm: Soft music *soothes* me. 2. To lessen pain or worry: A cool cream will *soothe* my sunburn. **soothed, soothing.**

speck·le (SPEK-əl) 1. A dot or small spot; a speck. 2. To dot with specks: My dress is *speckled* with green dots. **speckled, speckling.**

spike (SPIGHK) 1. A large, thick nail. 2. Any sharp, pointed object

that sticks out: Tulip *spikes* push up through the earth. 3. To join with a spike or put a spike into. **spiked, spiking.**

sprin·kle (SPRING-kəl) 1. To scatter in little bits or drops: *Sprinkle* some salt. 2. To rain slightly. 3. A small amount. 4. A light rain. **sprinkled, sprinkling.**

sput·ter (SPUHT-ər) 1. To make hissing, spitting noises. 2. To talk in a way that is difficult to understand. **sputtered, sputtering.**

squash (SKWOSH) 1. A fruit that grows on a vine and is used as a vegetable. 2. To crush or mash: Did you *squash* the strawberry on the floor? 3. The act or sound of squashing: I heard a *squash* when I stepped on the tomato. 4. A game played by hitting a ball against walls with rackets. **squashed, squashing.**

squawk (SKWAWK) 1. A loud harsh noise. 2. (Slang) A noisy complaint. 3. To make a loud harsh noise. 4. To complain. **squawked, squawking.**

squirm (SKWERM) To twist the body this way and that: I felt the worm *squirm* in my hand. **squirmed, squirming.**

squirt (SKWERT) To shoot out suddenly in a jet: This toy gun *squirts* water. **squirted, squirting.**

star·tle (STAHRT-l) To bring about sudden fright or movement; to surprise: We were *startled* by the noise in the woods. **startled, startling.**

steg·o·saur·us (STEG-ə-sor-əs) A plant-eating dinosaur having two rows of upright bony plates along its back.

stomp 1. To step or stamp heavily with the bottom of the foot: Everyone started to *stomp* to the music. 2. A heavy step or stamping. **stomped, stomping.**

stove·pipe (STOHV-pighp) 1. A metal pipe to carry smoke or fumes from a stove into the chimney. 2. A tall hat made of silk.

stud·y (STUHD-ee) 1. To try to learn: You must *study* for the test tomorrow. 2. To look at carefully: Babies *study* colorful objects. 3. A subject or field: Astronomy is the *study* of the stars, planets, and outer space. 4. A room used for reading or studying. **studied, studying, studies.**

sty (STIGH) 1. A pigpen. 2. A dirty place. **sties.**

su·per·vi·sor (SOO-pər-vigh-zər) One who directs or manages the work of others.

sup·ply (sə-PLIGH) 1. To furnish or provide: The school *supplies* pencils. 2. Goods or stock on hand or needed: Our paper *supplies* are kept in the cupboard. 3. The amount available: The demand for good housing is greater than the *supply.* **supplied, supplying, supplies.**

swamp (SWAHMP or SWAWMP) 1. Soft, wet land. 2. To sink; flood; fill with water: The big wave is going to *swamp* the boat. **swamped, swamping, swampy.**

swing 1. To move back and forth in a free swaying motion: The tree branches *swing* in the breeze. 2. A swinging movement, used to hit an object: She took a *swing* at the punching bag. 3. A seat, hung from above by chains or ropes, on which one moves back and forth through the air. **swung, swinging.**

switch (SWICH) 1. A stick used for whipping or beating. 2. Something to turn electricity on or off. 3. A change or shift. 4. To move back and forth like a switch: A horse *switches* its tail to chase the flies away. **switched, switching.**

tack·le (TAK-əl) 1. (Football) To jump on or seize in order to stop. 2. The act of tackling. 3. Something needed for special sports, especially fishing. 4. A position on a football team. **tackled, tackling, tackles.**

theme (THEEM) 1. The main idea in a story, play, or other work. 2. A short written story. 3. The main melody in a musical work.

thim·ble (THIM-bəl) A hard protective cap for the finger, worn while hand-sewing. **thimbles.**

thrash 1. To beat; give a whipping to. 2. To move (arms and legs)

tick

about in a forceful way: They saw the fish *thrash* in the water. **thrashed, thrashing.**

tick (TIK) 1. A sound made by a clock or a watch: The *tick* of the clock kept me awake. 2. To make the sound of a tick or ticks, as a clock does: We heard the insect *ticking* in the grass. **ticked, ticking.**

tin·gle (TING-gəl) 1. To feel a slight stinging, as from the cold, or a slap, or excitement: My fingers *tingle* from the cold. 2. A slight sting: The scary movie gave me a *tingle*. **tingled, tingling.**

tow·head (TOH-hed) A person with very light pale-yellow hair.

trach·o·don (TRAK-ə-don) A dinosaur with a long wide tail that lived in or near the water and ate only plants and leaves.

tri·cer·a·tops (trigh-SEHR-ə-tops) A dinosaur that ate only plants and leaves and had three horns on its head.

trom·bone (trom-BOHN) A brass musical instrument that has a sliding tube by means of which the player changes notes. **trombones.**

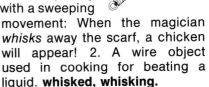

troop 1. A group of persons, animals, or things. 2. (Usually plural): A group of soldiers. 3. To go or walk, usually in a group: The students *troop* out of the classroom. **trooped, trooping.**

wobble

trout (TROWT) Any of a type of freshwater fish. **trout.**

ty·ran·no·sau·rus (ti-ran-ə-SAWR-uhss) A large flesh-eating dinosaur that walked on its hind legs.

vet Veterinarian. A doctor who cares for animals.

wade (WAYD) To walk through water or something that slows movement: They had to *wade* through mud to get to the other side. **waded, wading.**

wheel·bar·row (HWEEL-ba-roh) A container with a single wheel in front and two long handles in back, used for moving heavy loads.

whisk (HWISK) 1. (Used with *away, off,* or *out*) To grab, brush, or move quickly with a sweeping movement: When the magician *whisks* away the scarf, a chicken will appear! 2. A wire object used in cooking for beating a liquid. **whisked, whisking.**

wit 1. (Often plural) Ability to learn or understand: Jack used his *wits* when his little brother was bitten by a dog. 2. A sense of humor: Janice has a sharp *wit*. 3. A person with a good sense of humor.

wob·ble (WOB-əl) 1. To move from side to side in an unsteady way: Babies *wobble* when they start to walk. 2. An unsmooth movement. **wobbled, wobbling.**

BCDEFGHIJ 0854321
PRINTED IN THE UNITED STATES OF AMERICA